Introduction to this edition

Among the 'Big Four' companies the GWR was the only one to have survived the 1923 re-grouping of the railways with its name and territory intact. This gave the GWR a unique sense of continuity. And while its rivals – the LNER, LMS and Southern Railway – all produced various publications of their own, the GWR was able to build upon an established catalogue of railway books. Aside from the usual timetables this had begun with general guide books and the passenger/tourist angle was further exploited through publications such as *Through the Window*, the first volume of which covered the journey from Paddington to Penzance. Issued in 1924, and reprinted in 1927, it depicted the 300 mile route in the form of ribbon maps accompanied by information and illustrations on points of interest. By the late 1920s and into the 1930s other tourist-orientated titles appeared such as *The Cornish Riviera*, *Glorious Devon* and so on, as well as the annual *Holiday Haunts*.

The potential market for books aimed specifically at railway enthusiasts was not neglected. *GWR Names of Engines* appeared from 1911 onwards, and in 1923 *The 10.30 Limited* became the first in a series of 'Railway Books for Boys of All Ages'. A relatively thin volume of 136 pages, it nonetheless sold in the thousands and was quickly followed by *Caerphilly Castle* (1924), *The 'King' of Railway Locomotives* (1928) and the *Cheltenham Flyer* (1934). It was followed the follgoin year by *Track Topics*, which has also been reissued by Amberley publishing. Through these latter two publications, in particular, the enthusiasts could learn about the great locomotives – epitomosed by the Castle class featured in *Cheltenham Flyer* – as well as the minutiae of the engineering and operational aspects of the

railway; everything from the mail and freight services, safety appliance and the locomotive shops to building and maintaining the tracks, viaducts, bridges and tunnels. To my mind this makes them the most interesting of all of the GWR books. As you will see *Cheltenham Flyer* is divided into a series of talks and, in truth, the conversational style seems somewhat outmoded to the modern reader. For example, the first chapter begins with, 'Well, young fellow-me-lad ...' But bear with it for *Cheltenham Flyer* is packed with precious nuggets of useful and insightful information, much of it from a time when the railway was making the difficult transition from its Victorian origins to the fast-changing needs of the twentieth century.

By the 1930s the GWR had established a reputation for the quality of its advertising material, especially the posters designed by well known artists. This is reflected in the unattributed cover artwork for *Cheltenham Flyer* with its use of flat colour in a bold graphic style. The modern GWR 'button' logo places it firmly in the art deco era and this styling is carried through on the title page. It is a fascinating book, but as you dip into its pages remember that this is far more than just a nostalgia trip. After all, where else will you learn about fog precautions and transporting elephants, or the difference between inter-locking and track circuiting?

John Christopher

"CHELTENHAM FLYER"

A NEW RAILWAY BOOK

FOR BOYS OF ALL AGES

BY W. G. CHAPMAN

(*Author of " The* 10.30 *Limited," " The ' King ' of Railway Loco-motives," etc.*).

The main and original part of this book was published in 1934 by the Great Western Railway Company in the 'Boys of All Ages' series. Every effort has been made to produce this facsimile edition as faithfully as possible. For practical reasons the colour plate of the Flyer on the Maidenhead Bridge from the original is now opposite the contents page and in b+w. Likewise, the double-page map of the GWR network has been moved to the end of the book.

First published in 1934 by the GWR.
This edition by Amberley Publishing, 2014.

Amberley Publishing, The Hill, Stroud, Gloucestershire, GL5 4EP
www.amberley-books.com

Typesetting and origination by Amberley Publishing. Printed in the UK.

ISBN 978 1 4456 3481 4
E-book ISBN 978 1 4456 3502 6

FOREWORD

ORE than ten years ago a modest publication entitled " The 10.30 Limited " and subtitled " A Railway Book for Boys of All Ages " made its appearance. This was something of an experiment in railway literature, being an attempt to explain for the benefit of youthful admirers of our premier transport service, some of the more fascinating features of modern railway practice. The text took narrative form, descriptive of a train journey by the world-renowned " Cornish Riviera Express " of the Great Western Railway.

Launched with no little trepidation, " The 10.30 Limited " had a gratifying reception and four editions (72,000 copies) were called for in a space of six months. It was followed by three other publications in the " Boys of All Ages " series, two on the railway locomotive and one on docks and shipping. Of these four books, only the most recent—" The ' King ' of Railway Locomotives "—is now available.

Since the publication of " The 10.30 Limited " noteworthy, and in some cases epoch-making, developments have taken place in many phases of the railway industry—locomotives, carriages, wagons, signalling, train-control, permanent-way, etc. As a case in point, the average speed of " Cheltenham Flyer," now the world's fastest steam train, has actually increased during the past decade, by nearly ten miles an hour—from 61.8 to 71.3 !

FOREWORD

For some years past, requests have been received from railway enthusiasts for an up-to-date publication on the lines of the first and favourite volume in the " Boys of All Ages " series, and " Cheltenham Flyer " is an attempt to satisfy those demands.

For the sake of continuity, the " story " is told in narrative form, but the youngster for whom " The 10.30 Limited " was originally written, must fast be approaching man's estate. Perhaps, indeed, this book ought more appropriately to be dedicated to " *Men* of All Ages—particularly those under fourteen."

And having said so much by way of explanation and justification for " Cheltenham Flyer," it only remains to thank those readers who have so generously expressed appreciation of past efforts and to hope that they, together with new readers, will find this book to their liking.

W. G. C.

READING, 1934.

CHAPTERS

	The First	THE WORLD'S FASTEST TRAIN	*p.*	I
	The Second	SPEED—PROGRESS—ACHIEVEMENT		II
	The Third	" CORNISH RIVIERA EXPRESS "		23
	The Fourth	PADDINGTON OLD AND NEW		35

En Route
Paddington to Swindon (Chapters 5 to 15) :—

Paddington to Iver	The Fifth	HOW THE LOCOMOTIVE WORKS (1)	45
Iver to Taplow	The Sixth	HOW THE LOCOMOTIVE WORKS (2) —CLASSIFICATION OF LOCO- MOTIVES	55
Taplow to Reading	The Seventh	THE RAILWAY TRACK — STEEL SLEEPERS	65
Reading to Pangbourne	The Eighth	RAILWAY TICKETS—STREAMLINED RAIL CARS—SIGNALS	79
Pangbourne to Cholsey	The Ninth	LOCOMOTIVE WATER TROUGHS— HOW SIGNALS CONTROL TRAINS	91
Cholsey to Didcot	The Tenth	SIGNAL BOX EQUIPMENT—INTER- LOCKING—TRACK CIRCUITING, ETC.	101
Didcot	The Eleventh	AUTOMATIC TRAIN CONTROL— SAFETY APPLIANCES—FOG PRE- CAUTIONS	111
Didcot to Wantage Road	The Twelfth	STANDARD TIME—SINGLE LINES OF RAILWAY—COACHING STOCK	121
Wantage Road to Uffington	The Thirteenth	VACUUM BRAKE — EMERGENCY SIGNAL—SLIP COACHES	131
Uffington to Shrivenham	The Fourteenth	TRAIN LIGHTING AND HEATING	141
Shrivenham to Swindon	The Fifteenth	FREIGHT SERVICES — MAILS — NEWSPAPER TRAINS	151
	The Sixteenth	SWINDON—BUILDING LOCOMO- TIVES AND CARRIAGES—MILK TRANSPORT — THE " WHEEL TAPPER "	169
	The Seventeenth	SWINDON WORKS — CARRIAGE SHOPS	183
	The Eighteenth	SWINDON WORKS—LOCOMOTIVE SHOPS	191
	The Nineteenth	SWINDON WORKS—MORE LOCO- MOTIVE SHOPS	203
	The Twentieth	SWINDON TO LONDON BY "CHEL- TENHAM FLYER "	219

" Cheltenham Flyer " on record run

Photo : Topical Press.

THE WORLD'S FASTEST TRAIN

ELL, young fellow-me-lad, I understand you want to know something about the famous " Cheltenham Flyer "—the world's fastest train—and about the ways of steam railways generally. That's a pretty tall order, but orders of any kind are welcome in these days, and we'll see what can be done about it.

More than ten years ago, I may tell you, when you were probably taking more interest in rattles than in railways, another young hopeful came along here with a somewhat similar request. On that occasion it was possible to arrange to take him on a trip to Penzance by the Great Western Railway's famous " Cornish Riviera Express," more familiarly known since, to schoolboys, as " The 10.30 Limited." On the way we discussed many sides of railway working, and, I think I may say, got a fairly good idea of some of the " hows," " whys " and " wherefores." But that was some time ago, and our railways—particularly the Great Western Railway—have a very progressive policy, and much has happened since that time in many phases of railway activity.

I should like to vary the programme this time, and am hoping we can go together to Swindon, where, as perhaps you know, the locomotive, carriage, and wagon works of

I

the Railway are situated. We can have a chat about railways going down, look at some of the busy workshops
there, and then return to London on the world's fastest
train, " Cheltenham Flyer," in which you are so interested.

Such a programme will suit you, I hope. Good; but
we must remember that whilst we can chat about various
things as we travel *to* Swindon, neither you nor I can be
expected to concentrate our attention on much more than
the journey itself when speeding homewards at 80 miles
per hour ! Remember, too, that the run of $77\frac{1}{4}$ miles from
Swindon to Paddington takes but 65 minutes by " Cheltenham Flyer." No, I am afraid that train-journey was
not timed by the Great Western Railway for leisurely talks,
even on such fascinating subjects as railways provide, so
we must get in all we can before the homeward trip, which
is to be the thrill at the end—the jam after the pill, if you
like, but we will try and make the pill as palatable as
possible.

Now you are here, and as you seem so keenly interested
in " Cheltenham Flyer," perhaps you may like to hear a
little about this famous train before you actually make its
acquaintance.

Whilst it is only fitting that the country in which railways
were cradled, and which gave railways to the world, should
have the fastest train in the world, it is, I think you will
agree, equally fitting that the railway, which since its
earliest days has been noted for the speed of its trains,
should claim that record.

And, perhaps, before we go any further, I ought to make
it quite clear that by " railways " I mean *steam* railways in
all cases.

THE WORLD'S FASTEST TRAIN

Whilst " Cheltenham Flyer " has long been famous for its high speed, its story is one of steady acceleration. Before the war, it ran " non-stop " from Kemble Junction to Paddington—91 miles—in 103 minutes. When the war was over and normal services restored, a stop was put in at Swindon and 85 minutes allowed for the $77\frac{1}{4}$ miles run from there to Paddington. From July, 1923, the timing for the Swindon-Paddington run was reduced to 75 minutes or at an average speed of 61.8 miles per hour. At that speed it was the fastest " start to stop " run in the British Isles, and when in July, 1929, it was accelerated up to an average speed of 66.2 miles per hour—70 minutes being then allowed for doing the $77\frac{1}{4}$ miles—it took precedence of any other train in the wide world.

Such a claim, even when it came from a railway long renowned for high speeds, caused others to sit up and take notice, and our cousins overseas made up their minds to have a bold bid for the title. The result was that in April, 1931, the Canadian Pacific Railway timed one of its crack trains at an average speed of 68.9 miles an hour. With that timing, the record, of course, went from the Great Western Railway and Great Britain to the Canadian Pacific Railway and Canada.

But only for a few months was that much-coveted title to leave this country and the undertaking which had established it. The challenge was promptly taken up by the Great Western Railway, and in the following July " Cheltenham Flyer " was further accelerated to do the Swindon-Paddington trip at an average speed of 69.2 miles an hour.

This brought the record back to this country and there it remains, but that is not the whole story, for in September,

3

Log of " Cheltenham Flyer," June 6th, 1932

3.48 P.M. EXPRESS SWINDON TO PADDINGTON
(2.30 p.m. ex Cheltenham).
Engine 5006—" Tregenna Castle."   Type 4-cyl. 4–6–0.
Engine Crew: Driver Ruddock and Fireman Thorp.
Load : 6 coaches = 186 tons tare, 195 tons full.

miles.			min.	sec.	m.p.h.
0·0	SWINDON ..	start	0	00	—
1·0	Mile-post 76¼ ..	pass	2	10	—
2·0	„ 75¼ ..	„	3	15	64·3
3·0	„ 74¼ ..	„	4	09	69·2
4·0	„ 73¼ ..	„	4	58	75·0
5·0	„ 72¼ ..	„	5	45	78·9
5·7	Shrivenham ..	„	6	15	
7·3	Mile-post 70 ..	„	7	24	81·8
10·8	Uffington ..	„	9	51	
12·3	Mile-post 65 ..	„	10	56	84·9
13·4	Challow ..	„	11	42	
16·9	Wantage Road..	„	14	05	
17·3	Mile-post 60 ..	„	14	21	87·8
20·8	Steventon ..	„	16	40	
22·3	Mile-post 55 ..	„	17	41	90·0
24·2	DIDCOT ..	„	18	55	
27·3	Mile-post 50 ..	„	20	55	91·4
28·8	Cholsey ..	„	21	59	
32·3	Mile-post 45 ..	„	24	15	91·4
32·6	Goring	„	24	25	
35·8	Pangbourne ..	„	26	33	
37·3	Mile-post 40 ..	„	27	34	90·5
38·7	Tilehurst ..	„	28	28	
41·3	READING ..	„	30	12	
42·3	Mile-post 35 ..	„	30	51	91·4
46·3	Twyford ..	„	33	31	
47·3	Mile-post 30 ..	„	34	12	89·5
52·3	Mile-post 25 ..	„	37	38	87·4
53·1	Maidenhead ..	„	38	08	
57·3	Mile-post 20 ..	„	41	06	86·5
58·8	SLOUGH ..	„	42	10	
62·3	Mile-post 15 ..	„	44	36	85·7
64·1	West Drayton ..	„	45	51	
67·3	Mile-post 10 ..	„	48	13	82·9
68·2	SOUTHALL ..	„	48	51	
71·6	Ealing Broadway	„	51	17	
72·3	Mile-post 5 ..	„	51	48	83·7
75·3	Mile-post 2 ..	„	53	56	84·4
76·0	Westbourne Park	„	54	40	—
77·3	PADDINGTON	stop	56	47	—

1932, without the incentive of any further challenge, the Great Western Railway *again* improved upon its own world's record by reducing the time for " Cheltenham Flyer's " daily run from Swindon to Paddington from 70 to 65 minutes, giving the extraordinary average speed of 71.3 miles an hour for the whole trip of $77\frac{1}{4}$ miles !

Now, in so doing, the Great Western Railway not only broke its own wonderful world's record, but the new timing for the run at an average speed of 71.3 miles an hour was the very first occasion in the history of railways that any train had been regularly timed at over 70 miles an hour.

That was making history if you like and, just to mark the occasion of the introduction of the new record speed schedule, the train on its inaugural run covered the $77\frac{1}{4}$ miles from Swindon to Paddington in 61.08 minutes (instead of the new record schedule of 65), or, at an average speed of 75.98 miles an hour !

It is only fair, however, to record that on that run a speed restriction had to be observed at one point, where reconstruction work was in hand, but on a previous occasion the run had actually been made in 56 minutes 47 seconds, when a maximum speed of 91.4 miles an hour was achieved, and an average speed, for the whole trip, of 81.6 miles an hour !

You may be interested in the official log of such an historic run. Here it is, and it is well worth studying. As you see, 84 miles an hour and over was actually maintained (with the exception of quite brief falls to 82.9 and 83.7) from 12 miles from Swindon to within two miles of Paddington, whilst the highest speed (91.4 m.p.h.) was

5

" Cheltenham Flyer " and another

Photo: *London News Agency*

held for five miles at Cholsey and reached again between Reading and Twyford. It is, I expect, quite unnecessary to tell you that such a journey speed has never previously been equalled by steam, as far as railway records go.

The locomotives employed on this run are the Great Western Railway " Castles " which, in common with all G.W.R. express passenger locomotives, are built at the Company's Swindon Works, and as a further batch of these " greyhounds of the steel highway " is now under construction, we may see some of them in the making on our visit. The " Castles " are ten-wheeled engines (4-6-0) with a tractive effort of 31,625 lbs., and weigh with tender ready for the road about 126 tons.

The quantity of coal used on the Swindon-Paddington run is about 25 cwts., or 36 lbs. per mile. The water consumption is about 3,000 gallons and half of this is taken at speed from the Goring water troughs situated 33 miles from Swindon. We must look out for them on our trip.

Needless to say, the " road " is a favourable one for such a speedy run for, owing to the foresight of the Great Western Railway's first engineer, the celebrated I. K. Brunel, who made it originally for his broad gauge line, the track is nearly level. There is, as a matter of fact, a slight fall from Swindon to London, amounting to 270 feet, or less than the height of St. Paul's Cathedral on the whole $77\frac{1}{4}$ miles. The track is also without any severe curves.

That name " Cheltenham Flyer," by the way, seems to have been given to the train spontaneously by the press and public. " Why not Swindon Flyer ? " you may ask and " why not " ? Although the train does a good turn of speed throughout its journey from Cheltenham to London, it is, after all, on its run from Swindon to London that it makes its world record speeding.

I think the name is explained by the fact that trains from and to London get called after their destination and starting stations respectively—thus the 2.30 p.m. from Cheltenham (now 2.40 p.m.) would be known as the " Cheltenham " and when she earned her speed title by a special performance it was perhaps natural to add " Flyer " to the name. Anyway, " Cheltenham Flyer " she is and probably will remain.

I need not tell you that " Cheltenham Flyer " has made a name for herself all over the world and Americans, Chinese, Frenchmen, Germans, Indians and visitors from other countries have made a great point of including a trip on the world's fastest train in their itineraries.

One American visitor made the trip three times and gave it as his considered opinion that " it licked travelling by air into a cocked hat." Apparently the idea of " hitting London at 90 m.p.h." appealed strongly to him.

The train has been filmed and sound-recorded, from the air, the track, and also from the train itself. A footplate journey on the engine has been broadcast, as have the sounds of the train arriving and starting. One of the engine-drivers has flown in an aeroplane above the train on its journey and had the satisfaction of watching the " Flyer " speeding to London from quite a new angle.

On each occasion when the scheduled time has been reduced, the initial runs at a new record timing have created immense excitement all along the route. Crowds have gathered at stations and on bridges whilst railway enthusiasts, including "boys of all ages," have assembled at Paddington in their strength to cheer the " Flyer's " arrival and congratulate the engine crew. There is hardly a boys' paper that has not included in its exciting features a footplate trip by a quite imaginary and much-envied youth on the world's fastest train.

So great has been the interest in the train that special fares are put into operation, at certain times, for a journey to Swindon and thence to London by the " Flyer " and these tickets have been in continuous demand.

You have doubtless read something of the elaborate preparations that are made for record speed bids in the air, on the motor track, or on the water. How specially constructed machines are employed and manned by selected pilots or crews, while an expert staff is engaged in tuning up the engines for these great occasions.

" Cheltenham Flyer " gets none of this special treatment. It is a " start-to-stop " run—no flying start—and takes place each weekday as a matter of ordinary routine, summer and winter, shine or rain, using the same track as other trains which precede and follow it at short intervals all along its route.

The load behind the tender may vary from six to twelve coaches and its passenger freight may number anything up to 500, but that's all as may be; the " Flyer " still does her trip, and it's all in the regular day's work.

ONE UP TO STEAM.

EXHILARATED ANTIQUE (to delighted Shareholder):
"Eh, lad, but that's champion!"

(*A new railway record has been set up by the Cheltenham Express in its run from Swindon to Paddington.*)

SPEED—PROGRESS—ACHIEVEMENT

HE point I would here like to make is that "Cheltenham Flyer's" achievement with a *daily* scheduled run at an average speed of over seventy miles an hour for a 77 miles trip is in no way a "stunt" or something for which special preparations are made. Rather is it the result of close upon a century's development in the various departments of railway engineering and traffic organisation on the Great Western Railway. The engines and drivers doing this run are those on a regular roster just the same as for other trips, and the "Castle" locomotives employed are from a family of sixty, any one of which can take the "Flyer" over her ground in scheduled time.

Nor is speed a matter of locomotive power alone, as besides fast and powerful engines, a good sound track is essential, as also is modern signalling ; while to ensure that standard of comfort for passengers for which the Great Western Railway is renowned, well-constructed and comfortably-sprung rolling-stock behind the locomotive is no less important a factor.

And while "Cheltenham Flyer" is the fastest steam train in the world, it is only one of a large number of fast trains on the Great Western Railway, many of which run for considerable distances at high average speeds. Here is a list of some of them, and it should be noted that these are not all single trains, for there are four (2 each way) two-hour expresses between London and Bristol and no less than five between London and Birmingham, each week-day throughout the year.

	Distance Miles.		Time Mins.		Av'ge Speed m.p.h.
Swindon-London	77¼	..	65	..	71·3
Paddington-Bath	106¾	..	102	..	62·9
Paddington-Taunton ..	143	..	140	..	61·3
High Wycombe-Leamington	60¾	..	60	..	60·7
Paddington-Exeter	173¾	..	170	..	61·3
Paddington-Westbury ..	95½	..	95	..	60·3
Paddington-Bristol (*via* Bath)	118¼	..	120	..	59·2
Bristol-Paddington (*via* Bad-minton)	117½	..	120	..	58·8
Paddington-Leamington ..	87¼	..	90	..	58·2
Paddington-Torquay ..	199¾	..	210	..	57·1
Banbury-Paddington ..	67½	..	71	..	57·0
Paddington-Plymouth ..	225¾	..	240	..	56·4
Paddington-Birmingham ..	110½	..	120	..	55·2

As you will see, this list includes runs of over 200 miles at average speeds approaching the mile-a-minute rate, while all the times included have an average speed of over 55 miles an hour.

ᔕ ᔕ ᔕ ᔕ

There can surely be no finer prelude to a holiday, and few things really more restful, than a long journey by express train in this year of grace. Ensconced in a comfortable seat the passenger can either read or write, smoke or sleep, or just watch the glorious panorama of our countryside unroll before him, as the train glides smoothly and swiftly to its destination. When the inner-man calls for refreshment he will find an appetising meal, daintily served, awaiting him in the dining car and, if taking a night journey, he can " turn in " in a well appointed sleeping-car at his starting place, sleep soundly and awaken rested and refreshed at his destination.

That is railway travel to-day, and it is the product of a century of steady progress, although there are critics who tell us that there has been little improvement in train speeds during the past fifty years. That statement, of course, like so many misleading assertions, is partly true, but speed must not be compared with speed alone. High speed trains have always been a feature of Great Western Railway travel, and reference to Bradshaw's time-table of 1848—but eight years after the railway reached Swindon —shows that trains were timed from London to Swindon with two stops at 54.35 miles an hour or, excluding stops, at 61.60 miles an hour. That was eighty-six years ago, and such a speed was admittedly greater than anything known at the time. There were, in fact, Great Western Railway trains in 1848 whose scheduled time was 57 miles an hour, and in that same year there are records of a special run when 68 miles an hour was attained, but (and the *but* is a big one), creditable as these speeds undoubtedly were, train loads in those days were only a fraction of what they are to-day. Trains of four, five, or six small four- or six-wheeled coaches were usual then, whilst to-day, the load behind the tender may be anything up to fourteen, or even more, eight-wheeled corridor coaches with kitchen and dining cars.

Another point to be borne in mind when making speed comparisons with earlier days, is the increased congestion of the running lines and the greater precautions which have

Bristol-Paddington Express approaching Swindon (Locomotive "King George V.")

necessarily to be taken for safely working the long and heavy trains which follow one another so closely over the rails to-day.

The general average speed of express trains on the Great Western Railway is remarkably high and the " Cornish Riviera Express" is an example of a heavy train which daily accomplishes a " non-stop " run over as difficult a road as is to be found on any trunk line in this country at an average of 56½ miles an hour. Perhaps the best evidence of progress in railway practice is to be found in a comparison between that train in 1904 (when it was inaugurated) and 1934, as set out in this table. You will see the weight of the engine has increased from 92 tons to nearly 136 tons, the coaches from seven to fourteen in number, and their empty weight from 182 to 480 tons, seating capacity from 268 to 496 and dining capacity from 50 to 86 passengers and, despite all that, the journey time has been very substantially reduced, even allowing for the shorter route.

You probably know that the Great Western Railway is a railway of many records—particularly in the matter of speeds. It was a G.W.R. Ocean Mails Special drawn by locomotive " City of Truro " (4-4-0) which, as long ago as 1904, achieved the highest speed (102.3 miles) ever recorded by a railway train. That was on a journey from Plymouth to Bristol, after passing Whiteball Tunnel, and the record has stood unassailed for 30 years. It is a story which I don't propose to tell again, but you may be interested to learn what is not so generally known, that the engine " Duke of Connaught " (one of the old 7 ft. 8 ins. single-wheelers), which took the train on from Bristol to Paddington, not only did the trip of 118 miles 33 chains in less than 100 minutes and arrived perfectly cool in every

Cornish Riviera Express

COMPARATIVE DATA 1904 AND 1934

	1904	1934
LOCOMOTIVE—		
CLASS - - -	" City "	" King "
NO. OF CYLINDERS -	Two (18in. x 26in.)	Four (16¼in. x 28in.)
WHEEL ARRANGEMENT -	4–4–0	4–6–0
TRACTIVE EFFORT -	17,790 lbs.	40,300 lbs.
(at 85 per cent. B.P.)		
WEIGHT (with tender) -	92 tons 1 cwt.	135 tons 14 cwt.
LENGTH (with tender) -	56 ft. 4¾ ins.	68 ft. 2 ins.
COACHES—		
LENGTH - - -	54 ft. to 58 ft.	60 ft.
WIDTH (outside)- -	8 ft. 6¾ ins.	9 ft. 7 ins.
WEIGHT - - -	25 tons	35 tons
NUMBER OF COACHES ON		
TRAIN - - -	7	14
TOTAL WEIGHT (behind		
tender) - -	182 tons	480 tons
SEATING - - -	268	496
ILLUMINATION - -	Gas	Electric
ILLUMINATION (natural)-	Ordinary Window Glass	" Vita " Glass (admitting ultra-violet rays)
DINING CAPACITY -	50	86
HEATING - - -	Steam pipe	2 radiators per compartment
ROOFS - - -	Clerestory	Elliptical (greater air space)
GENERAL CONSTRUCTION	Wood	Wood framing and steel panelling
COMPARTMENTS :—		
Length, 1st Class -	7 ft. 0 ins.	7 ft. 6 ins.
„ 3rd „ -	5 ft. 6 ins.	6 ft. 4½ ins.
Width, 1st and 3rd		
Class - -	5 ft. 9 ins.	6 ft. 8¾ ins.
CORRIDOR DOORS -	Swing	Sliding
TIME OCCUPIED—		
LONDON TO PLYMOUTH -	4 hrs. 25 mins	4 hours
„ PENZANCE -	7 hours	6 hrs. 25 mins.
ROUTE - - -	*Via* Bristol	*Via* Castle Cary (saving 19 miles)

bearing, but actually took an express train *back* to Bristol two hours after bringing in the mail train !

It is difficult to mention those speedy old single-wheelers of the G.W.R. without referring to the earlier broad gauge flyers. They made a great name for speed and it is said that one of the drivers solemnly offered to attempt a run of 118¼ miles, London to Bristol, in an hour, and thoroughly believed he could do so if permitted, though history seems to be quite silent as to the result of such a sporting offer.

Those engines were booked to leave Didcot (53 miles from Paddington) 57 minutes after their departure from Paddington, allowing for a stop at Didcot, and they repeatedly did the run in 50 minutes, often in less.

Those old flyers must have been handsome indeed, with their large driving wheels, brass-mounted boilers and wheel covers. " Lord of the Isles," built in 1851, perhaps the most famous of the old 8 ft. " single-wheelers," was continuously in service until 1884 with her original boiler intact. Here is a photograph of her and it is of particular interest because it shows the seat in use in those days by the " travelling porter " on the tender facing the train. The duty of this porter was to warn the driver if anything happened to the train.

If you want some idea of the progress in locomotive engineering on the Great Western Railway, you might usefully compare " Lord of the Isles "—one of the crack locomotives of its time—with a modern G.W.R. passenger engine such as a " Castle " or " King." Incidentally, I may add that the tractive effort (at 85 per cent. boiler pressure)—which is the basis of comparing locomotive

" Lord of the Isles "

power—has increased from 9,640 lbs. for " Lord of the Isles " to 31,625 lbs. for the " Castle," and 40,300 lbs. for the " King " locomotives.

And I think we can truthfully say that progress and development in locomotive engineering on the Great Western Railway is typical of the whole undertaking.

A railway is a vast and complex system and railway progress is not, of course, merely a matter of speed or of better mechanical equipment. It is also in large measure the result of improved organisation (and all that involves), based on experience, more efficient traffic working and the extension of increased facilities to the travelling and trading public.

We'll have a talk about the mechanical side of the business on our trip to Swindon, and though I know you're more interested in locomotives and signals and how they work, you may like to know a little about what has been done to date in, say, the matter of facilities for the railway passenger.

Well, to start with, I think I can say that if any irritating restrictions may have existed in regard to railway travel in the past they have now been swept away for good and all.

18

On the Great Western Railway, to-day, if you take a third class " summer " ticket (which costs about one-third less than the ordinary fare) you can, for instance, travel by any train in the time-table in either direction, on any day (provided you return within one calendar month) and you can break your journey both " out " and " home " if you like. If you wish, you can travel by " Cheltenham Flyer," " Cornish Riviera Express," " Torbay Limited " or any of the many other fast expresses, and I particularly mention this because I think I am right in saying that Great Britain is about the only large country in which supplementary fares are *not* demanded for travel by the fastest trains.

But a third class " summer " ticket includes more than this, for if it covers places served by the London, Midland and Scottish or the London and North Eastern Railways, it is available for the return journey—as are ordinary return, tourist tickets, etc.—by any of the recognised routes of those railways, if so desired.

Through cross-country trains have been considerably increased of recent years, and passengers using more than one railway company's lines can now travel by through coach from home station to distant destinations in a large number of cases. Examples of this much-appreciated facility are the through services between Birkenhead, Chester, Shrewsbury and the Midlands, and Margate, Dover, Folkestone, Hastings, Brighton, etc., over the Great Western and Southern Railways; and those between Bradford, Leeds, Sheffield and Northern towns, and Bournemouth and Southampton over the London and North-Eastern, Great Western, and Southern Railways, to quote only two

" Cornish Riviera Express " between Dawlish and Teignmouth

from quite a large number of such through services. Perhaps the most remarkable cross-country run is that between Aberdeen and Penzance, *via* Edinburgh, York, Sheffield, Banbury and Swindon, and *vice versa*—a distance of 800 miles. You have only to look at your map of Great Britain to see the full extent of these facilities.

Other features which have contributed to the " joy of the journey " by railway are registered seats, " luggage-in-advance," and the extension of restaurant-car facilities, whilst the increasing habit of taking rail tickets in advance at town or city offices has reduced anxiety on the part of the passenger, and together these have made railway travel the care-free and enjoyable experience that it is to-day.

Yes, the railways have done much to improve travel, but they also deserve the support of our countrymen because they are amongst the largest employers in the country, and the largest contributors to local rates, as well as the greatest consumers of British products, including coal. In these days, it is well to remember that our railways— which throughout every hour of the day and night are actively employed in serving the needs of our people—are British to the backbone. The locomotives, carriages and wagons, like the rails over which they run are made of British steel and they derive their motive power from British coal.

ʊ   ʊ   ʊ   ʊ

Well, that's enough, I think, for the moment. But if your engagements permit, we might manage our trip to Swindon to-morrow.

So shall we say 10.15 a.m. at Paddington Station. We had better meet under the big clock on No. 1 Platform. How will that do? . . Splendid! Till to-morrow then.

PADDINGTON STATION No. 1 PLATFORM

"CORNISH RIVIERA EXPRESS"

ONGRATULATIONS on your punctuality, for I see our three-faced friend above says exactly 10.15. For the next six or seven hours I want you to keep your eyes and ears open and I think I can promise that you will see and hear much of interest on your favourite subject.

There was a motive in getting you here at this time, and I thought, before setting out on our own journey, we might have a look at the "Cornish Riviera Express," now standing at the platform. Personally, I always get a thrill from the departure of "the 10.30" which leaves this platform daily on its wonderful run at high speed to our most westerly town of Penzance—a run without a pause for breath until it reaches Plymouth (226 miles distant) in four hours.

If we work forward from the back of the train to the engine, we ought to arrive there in good time before she ſtarts ; so let's begin our inspeċtion in the rear.

It is pretty evident that moſt of these happy passengers are going to the Weſt Country for holidays, and looking forward to their journey. There is real romance about a train which daily transports from this old London of ours so many who, for a few weeks, are exchanging the routine of the work-a-day world for rolling moors, rugged coaſts, fern clad lanes, and all the charms of the Weſt. Doubtless they are eagerly anticipating all the fun, frolic, and freedom in and by the sea, and on those glorious beaches where the health-giving Atlantic breezes work such wonders. I'm sure we should see a great change in their appearance could we be present when they return from their holidays.

Passengers are moving to their regiſtered seats on the train, and porters are busy with luggage, although I may tell you that the holiday passenger of to-day is making greater use of the " luggage-in-advance " service which cuts out all bother on the journey.

These last two coaches are labelled Weymouth, and are slipped *en route* at Westbury ($95\frac{1}{2}$ miles) whilſt the train proceeds without ſtopping on its journey. That special tail lamp, red and white, on the laſt coach tells the signal-men along the route that a slip portion is to be detached.

On the front of the firſt of these two coaches we see the slip hook, and if you take a peep into that compartment, which is occupied by the slip-guard, you will see the lever by means of which he operates the slipping apparatus, which cuts off these two coaches from the main train.

The coaches of the train are, of course, arranged in the

order in which they are to be put off, and the next two, as you see, are labelled for Newquay, then one Falmouth and the next for St. Ives, whilst the rest of the train, which consists of eight coaches, including two dining cars, works through to Penzance.

So you see, the whole train on its summer service formation consists of fourteen vehicles, behind the tender, and that represents a load (without passengers and luggage) of 480 tons. As there is seating for 496 passengers, the total loaded weight is round about 550 tons. In times of pressure the load may be increased to sixteen coaches, weighing 545 tons without passengers or luggage.

The coaches, which are of fireproof material, are 60 feet long and 9 ft. 7 ins. wide—the widest in the country. The train is electrically lighted throughout, and electric fans and air extractors are fitted in the dining saloons ; in fact, the furnishing and equipment of this famous train are just about the last word in travel comfort. I wish we had time to inspect it more closely, but I know you are itching to get along to the locomotive and we must move onwards, but perhaps I ought to mention that these coaches are glazed with Vita glass, which admits the health-giving ultra-violet rays of the sun, which ordinary glass excludes. No wonder the " Cornish Riviera Express " has been called " the aristocrat of railway trains " !

It's a longish walk from one end of the train to the other, but here we are and here is the fine locomotive. Meet " King Richard I " (No. 6027).

From your point of view, I can see we have left the *pièce de résistance* to the last, and I must admit that I quite share your ardent admiration of the " King " locomotives.

26

"CORNISH RIVIERA EXPRESS"

They are without doubt worthy of their name for they are the perfect embodiment of majestic power and dignity. That beautiful, long-tapered boiler, the squat copper-topped funnel, and the huge driving wheels, seem to suggest strength, speed, and reliability.

The shining green and black livery of G.W.R. passenger locomotives, relieved by the polished brass and copper, gives them a really spick-and-span appearance, and in the sunlight this morning " King Richard I " looks as if " she " (we cannot call locomotives " he," even if they are " Kings ") had just completed a wonderful toilet—as indeed she has.

It is rather strange to think that this latest type of passenger locomotive is the lineal descendant of the first railway engine, built by Trevethick in 1802 and which was the father of the whole race. G.W.R. locomotives have a particularly noble and distinguished ancestry, for they come from a stock which produced such old-time flyers as " Lord of the Isles " and have among their later forbears the famous " Dukes," " Bulldogs," " Cities " and " Counties," while the " Saints," " Stars," " Halls " and " Castles " are the sisters of the " Kings."

You are, I know, envying the driver and fireman, and who can help it ? The fascination and glamour which surrounds the railway locomotive extends to the engine crew, and whilst theirs is a responsible and trustworthy calling, it is also surely something of a privilege to have the control of such a noble example of modern locomotive engineering at the head of what one writer has called " The Wonder Train to the West." To be in charge of this train is indeed one of the " high spots " (as they say in the " talkies ") of the craft.

" Cornish Riviera Express " leaving Paddington

"CORNISH RIVIERA EXPRESS"

What is the secret of the charm and fascination of the steam locomotive for boys of all ages, do you think ? Ever since there have been railways, there have been young railway enthusiasts (and some not so young) who were keenly interested in everything about locomotives, and this despite the lure of electricity and other modern scientific inventions. There must be a "something" about the steam locomotive to inspire such admiration, almost affection, for it seems to be entirely wanting in the electric locomotive, be it ever so powerful. Perhaps it is that the steam locomotive developing its own energy and not being dependent upon distant power stations, has more of a "personality"—shall we say ? Whatever it is, and however difficult it is to define, it certainly exists, and in the party now gathered round and doing homage to "King Richard I" we have first hand evidence of the fact, if indeed any is needed.

Both driver and fireman now seem quite satisfied that everything on their beloved engine is in perfect order for the trip. For some time they have been opening a cock here, testing something there, looking to the oil-cups and so on, but now both are on the *qui vive* for their signal is "off," and they only await the "right-away" from the rear of the train. The passengers have taken their seats and friends are grouped round the carriage doors exchanging farewells. . . .

There goes the whistle for which the driver has been waiting, and to which he responds with a shrill note from the engine, as with steady hand he partly opens the regulator. As he does so steam rushes into the four huge cylinders, and the mighty pistons and driving wheels come

29

to life. Before we realise it, this long train is gliding out of Paddington Station—ever so gently at first, but gradually accelerating, to an accompaniment of last messages, promises to " be sure and write," and fluttering handkerchiefs ; starting once again on her daily run over the romantic route to " the delectable duchy "—at 10.30 a.m. precisely.

Let's give her a wave. . . .

∽   ∽   ∽   ∽

As I said, there is always a thrill about the departure of " the 10.30 " and I am sure you can share in it this morning. She is off " non-stop " to Plymouth and then on to Penzance, while half-an-hour ago—at 10.0 a.m.—to-day as every weekday, the Up " Cornish Riviera Express " left Penzance for Paddington. These two trains will pass one another on that glorious stretch of line which runs alongside the sea, at Dawlish Warren, at 1.29 p.m.

Did you know that the " non-stop " run of this train from London to Plymouth was a world's record when it was instituted just thirty years ago, when nothing of the kind had ever been attempted in a regular service before ? That record was maintained for nearly a quarter of a century without challenge, with the exception of some adjustments due to national requirements during the war period, and the average speed maintained on the run is still higher than any other " non-stop " train run of over 200 miles in the country.

The " Cornish Riviera Express " was also unique for many years in that, during the winter service, it carried three slip portions detached at speed at Westbury, Taunton and Exeter respectively.

"CORNISH RIVIERA EXPRESS"

During the summer service this train now runs " non-stop " London to Plymouth in 4 hours. The throughout journey, London to Penzance, takes 6 hours 25 minutes.

A stop is now made at Exeter during the winter service, when slips for Westbury and Taunton are carried. The timing London to Plymouth (including the stop) is then only 4 hours 4 minutes for the 226 miles.

So popular is this train that during the summer months it frequently runs in two parts on Saturdays whilst on Saturdays preceding Bank Holidays it may run in two, three, or four separate parts ; in fact it has, on occasion, been necessary on the Saturday before August Bank Holiday—the day of the big holiday exodus—to run no fewer than five " Cornish Riviera Expresses " to convey the large numbers of holiday makers who select Sunny Cornwall as their vacation resort.

A Scene at Paddington Station in 1862

Paddington Station, by the way, is just eighty years old, and although there have been many extensions and alterations during that time, much, including the beautiful arched roof, is part of Brunel's original design. If you visited the Exhibition of British Art at the Royal Academy recently you doubtless saw Frith's " Railway Station " (No. 626) and will recognise the graceful roof spans which

From the painting by W. P. Frith, R.A.

figured in the picture. These are just as they were in 1854, although you may be surprised to hear that the original pillars which supported the roof have all been replaced. The actual lamp cases which are such a conspicuous feature in Frith's picture survived until 1904. Speaking of lighting, it may interest you to know that Paddington was the first station to be lighted by arc lamps.

Train Indicator on the "Lawn" at Paddington Station

PADDINGTON—OLD AND NEW

T HE tumult and the shouting have died— the captains and the " King " departed, as we return along No. 1 platform and meet the shunting engine that brought in the empty train, and is now impatiently seeking its release.

The vacant line of rails looks rather ſtrange at firſt, and the platform is clearing as those who have speeded the holiday-makers on their way retire. This clearing gives us an opportunity to admire what is probably unique among war memorials. It commemorates the 2,524 G.W.R. men who gave their lives in the Great War. The momument consiſts of a bronze figure of a " Tommy " not in any martial pose, but with his great coat thrown carelessly over his shoulders reading a letter. Unconventional, perhaps, but appropriate and quite typical of so many thousands who gave all for their Country.

ᔆ   ᔆ   ᔆ   ᔆ

We have been hearing a lot about depressions of late years—in faƈt the word seems to have been much overworked whether the depressions are personal or Icelandic in origin, or whether they concern world trade. After all, mere talking about a trouble is no remedy for it. Although the Great Western Railway has suffered like a good many others from the abnormal conditions that have prevailed during the past three or four years, those in authority have not sat down and waited for better times, but taken the view that a temporary falling off in business, bad as it has been (and still is), provided an opportunity for carrying out a scheme of development and modernisation of equipment, so that the railway would be able more efficiently to deal with the traffic which must accompany an ultimate trade revival. Besides hoping for better times they have been working for them.

The Great Western was the first of the railways to take advantage of the financial assistance offered by the Government to those undertaking works schemes in order to ease the burden of unemployment. More than forty such works schemes have been undertaken and include extensive re-constructions at Paddington, Bristol, Cardiff and other stations and (among other large works) quadrupling of an important length of the line on the route to the West. A number of dock improvements have also been carried

War Memorial,
Paddington Station

out; no fewer than 5,000 twenty-ton mineral wagons are being built, whilst in addition the G.W.R. system of automatic train control and audible signalling, which had been installed on certain sections of the railway, has now been extended over two thousand miles of main line.

ᔕ   ᔕ   ᔕ   ᔕ

But let's have a quick look round Paddington Station and see something of the improvements which have been carried out here, at a cost of approximately a million pounds, before our train for Swindon leaves from No. 2 Platform at 10.45 a.m. The Paddington improvements included the remodelling of the whole of the track for over three-quarters of a mile and resignalling by power operated and colour light signals as well as building alterations.

Passing down the platform we come to the large circulating area behind the ends of the rails known as the " lawn," and resplendent in new paint. This part of the station has just undergone complete transformation, and in fact, all you can now see in that direction is brand new. The new works include two multi-storied blocks of offices, one on each side of lawn, and have involved the transfer of the Parcels Depôt from the lawn to the other end of the station, where yet another block of offices has been provided above it.

But I really must beg your pardon; I see the term "lawn" is puzzling you, and no wonder. Some time ago a story was being told about an enterprising salesman who, over-hearing some conversational reference to an " extension of the lawn at Paddington Station," journeyed post-haste to the G.W.R. headquarters in the fond hope of selling

37

New Offices, Arrival Approach Road, Paddington Station

the Authorities a motor lawn-mower for grooming their greensward ! There is no point, of course, in such a yarn, unless you know Paddington Station, for what is known as the " lawn " by every railwayman employed here and also by a good many of the public who use the station regularly, is this large covered area now before you, about as little like a lawn as anything it is possible to imagine.

" The Lawn at Paddington Station " has been the subject of an article in one of our daily papers, which stated on some authority, presumably, that it was a survival from the time when " a garden stood on the site with its roof overhead." Some wag has even suggested that the explanation of the term is to be found in the use of the words " Van-in " and " Van-out " when the parcels and carts worked to and from this site ! More than likely there was a lawn here before the present station and hotel (which lies beyond the " lawn ") were built and the name carried on ever since. Anyway the survival is strange.

The " lawn " of to-day is a circulating area of about an acre in extent and a vast improvement to the station. In the offices you see in the background, over the entrance to and exit from the Underground Railways, are housed the Publicity staff of the Railway, which is responsible, among other things, for the various publications issued by the Company.

Here, on the lawn, is something which, I am sure, will intrigue you. It is a new type of electric train indicator, quite recently installed, and the only one of its kind in the world.

As you see, there are on the " arrival " side eight panels in each of which is shown the arrival time of a train, the number of platform at which it will be received, whether it is running late, and if so, how late, and the principal

39

stations it has served. On the reverse side is displayed a list of departures. An electrically controlled clock faces in each direction, so that all necessary information regarding movements of trains is available at one central spot.

The indicator is controlled from an office some distance away, and is not visible to the operator, but a miniature panel, which gives the operator similar information to that displayed by the indicator, is provided in the control office.

The indicator is a marvellous piece of electrical apparatus, and it is most fascinating to watch the changes on the arrival side, and see the particulars regarding one train " washed out," and those of another appear, as if by magic, in their place.

In the right-hand corner of the lawn where you now see those G.P.O. men with bags of mails, is the conveyor which connects with what is perhaps the most wonderful of underground railways. It was built at a cost of one and a half million pounds to carry His Majesty's mails between the Eastern District Post Office, Whitechapel and Paddington. Fourteen years were spent on the construction of this six-and-a-half miles long and eighty feet deep railway. The whole operation of the railway is automatic. The trains, which can travel at 35 miles an hour and deal with a peak load of 45 tons of mails an hour, have no drivers or conductors, but are controlled by operators seated in cabins at each of the nine stations. Such is the wizardry of this G.P.O. railway. During the war when work on the railway was suspended, some of the most valuable treasures of the British Museum were housed for safety from air attack in this Post Office railway tube.

But time is getting on and, if you doubt it, come and

have a look at this newest thing in time recorders, which has been erected by Messrs. Whiteleys, whose store is nearby. Its proper name is a " chronoscope " and it is the largest in the world. You see without dial or hands it records the exact time, minute by minute, in big figures, which change in a most fascinating way before your eyes. The time, by the way, is electrically synchronised with the other 200 clocks at Paddington Station which take Greenwich mean time from a master clock in the Telegraph Office.

Now we will go a few yards up the Arrival Approach Road and glance at one of the two big blocks of offices which I mentioned a moment or two ago. . . . There it is, a fine example of modern architecture and building, only quite recently completed. Those huge letters " G.W.R. Paddington " can be flood-lighted from below as you see. Here on the ground floor are spacious refreshment and dining rooms.

From the roof of this building of eight floors a wonderful view of London is obtainable on a clear day, but I am afraid you will have to take my word for that, for the time being at any rate, as we must be moving towards our train.

The view we get of the station, platforms, etc., as we retrace our steps (with our backs to the lawn) is much as it was ten years ago, but the departure platforms have all been considerably extended northwards and a new over-bridge connecting them provided. This station now has well over three miles of platform frontages. Bishops Road Station, which adjoined Paddington at the north end, has disappeared as a separate structure, and now comes under the same roof, and the new platforms provided deal with suburban trains as well as through G.W.R. services to the City and the Hammersmith and City and Metropolitan Railway trains. It is, in fact, at the two ends of the station particularly that the new works, which have been going on so energetically in recent years, are to be seen.

About 140 trains are despatched from Paddington main station and 255 from the Suburban side (30 steam and 225 electric) every twenty-four hours ; the number leaving the main station on a busy Saturday in the holiday season is 190 and about the same number of trains arrive.

I will say nothing about the despatch of newspaper trains from Paddington just now, as I want to include the subject in our chat on railway matters a little later on.

Every day, 2,700 churns of milk arrive here, or 986,300 churns annually, the same number being despatched empty, and about 30,000 tons of fish are unloaded at the station in the year, as much as 500 tons being handled in a single morning. As much as 370 tons of perishable fruit (in 17,500 packages) for Covent Garden Market has also been dealt with here in one day.

These items are entirely independent of the general parcels traffic, of which there are about 17,500 packages outwards and 15,000 inwards daily, besides His Majesty's mails, theatrical scenery, "boxes" of horses, and so forth.

About 1,500 taxi-cabs enter the station daily, and hardly a day passes when there is not something of special interest to be seen. Celebrities arriving or leaving, and so on. And that reminds me that unless we hustle, two " celebrities " will lose their train for Swindon.

Yes, we really must hurry. There's our train. I want to make a purchase at the bookstall—so skip along and secure a compartment.

Preparing for the run—

Cleaning and Watering the Engine

Interested Young Railway Enthusiasts

HOW THE LOCOMOTIVE WORKS—(1)

STOUT fellow! You've bagged seats in a smoker, and I appreciate the kind thought. You had better have that corner facing the engine, and I can sit here opposite you.

I expect you noticed that the non-smoking as well as the smoking compartments are labelled. That is a fairly recent innovation, and I mention it because a boy visitor from across the Channel, who had been staying here, was much interested in our railways, particularly the G.W.R., and in writing home he told his people that the Great Western not only held the speed records and had the most powerful locomotives, but that the coaches were reserved for " Ladies," " Smoking," " No Smoking," " Reading," and even the " Bath." There's a testimonial for you !

But I haven't shown you my bookstall purchase. Here it is. Three books which I think you will find interesting and all are about G.W.R. engines. This one is *The ' King ' of Railway Locomotives*, which gives the story of

45

"CHELTENHAM FLYER"

G.W.R. engines from the earliest days to the "Kings," and describes their construction and so forth. This album, *Locomotives of the Great Western Railway*, consists, as you see, of a dozen photogravure plates, of different types of engines, with dimensions, etc.; and here is the popular *G.W.R. Engine Book*, which contains the names and numbers, types and classes of G.W.R. locomotives, with lots of photographs and detailed descriptions. As there is so much to say in so short a time you'll like to have these as they will amplify what we shall have to say about the locomotive. I can already see that the engine is your favourite railway topic as it is of so many boys of all ages.

Have a look through them, while I get my pipe under weigh and then I shall have something to say on several railway matters as we proceed. I have brought some photographs and diagrams to assist you. . . .

Hello! we are off. Take a look out on the left and right, if you can, as we leave the station and you will see some of the alterations I spoke of at this end. There on the right are the suburban platforms—of the late Bishops Road Station, and you will notice how all the main line platforms have been newly lengthened. Now look out on the left and you'll see the new parcels depôt, removed from the lawn. There is also a new subway from that depôt with automatic electric lifts to the station platforms.

If you look out along the line you will see that the familiar semaphore signals have disappeared and been completely replaced by colour-light signals. This has been done all the way from Paddington to Southall. We will have something to say about this innovation when discussing signalling later on and also about the new signal boxes at Paddington Station.

HOW THE LOCOMOTIVE WORKS

The electric train on the right is travelling from the City to Addison Road (the station for Olympia) and it will pass under the Great Western Main Lines by subway directly and come to the surface again on this side of Westbourne Park Station. That big signal box is known as Subway Junction Box, and on a normal day about 790 trains and engines pass it. At the peak of the holiday season, or a busy Saturday in summer, the number is increased by a hundred, or an average of about thirty-seven trains and engines pass the box every hour.

We are accelerating now, and at the depôt over on your right you see railwaymen busily dealing with the modern road-rail container traffic, a sign of the times in this changing world. We pass Westbourne Park Station and under the skew bridge, by means of which light engines and empty coaching stock cross the running lines from and to the extensive carriage and locomotive sheds at Old Oak Common. There they are on the right, and it is there that the rolling stock for Paddington Station is stabled. That reminds me that we must get on with our railway talk but I might just say that the line you now see going off to the right is the route to Birmingham, and many of the express trains do the 110 miles from London to the great Midland City and *vice versa* in two hours.

Where shall we start our railway talks ? . . . With the locomotive, you think. . . . Very well then, here we go !

ᔕ   ᔕ   ᔕ   ᔕ

You know, of course, that the locomotive converts water into steam and steam into power, and that heat is generated by burning coal in the fire-box of the boiler. The heat

Paddington " Suburban " Station (late Bishop's Road)

thus produced is transferred to water which surrounds the fire-box and boiler tubes through which the hot gases pass ; the water thus being turned into steam. The steam is, of course, the medium for storing and carrying the heat to the cylinders of the locomotive where it is transformed into power.

The steam, which is super-heated and governed by a regulator valve, is distributed by valves in the steam-chest to the cylinders, causing the pistons to move to and fro.

Don't bother your head about *how* it is done for a moment, but I want you to look closely at this photograph which explains more clearly than anything I can say how the " to-and-fro " motion obtained at the pistons (we will see just *how* presently) is transformed into rotary motion at the driving wheels. As you see, a rod which passes through the back cover of the cylinder (the piston rod), is attached to the piston, and this rod is secured to a block sliding between two guide bars and known as a " crosshead "—all clearly marked in the photograph. To the crosshead is attached, by a pin passing through it, a connecting rod, the other end of which is secured to a pin in the driving wheel a short distance from the axle centre. Now we have got piston—piston rod—crosshead—connecting-rod—axle pin—driving wheel—all connected up in that order, and I think you will easily see how, when steam moves piston, piston moves rod, rod moves crosshead, etc., etc.—like the old woman getting her pig over the style in your nursery days—the reciprocating or " to-and-fro " motion at the cylinder is converted into rotary motion at the driving wheels. You see our locomotive is getting a move on.

Here we are making a brief stop at Ealing Broadway Station and over on your right you can see the " tube " trains of the Ealing & Shepherds Bush Line and beyond them the trains of the District Railway. But we are off again, and soon on the Wharncliffe Viaduct, which spans the Brent Valley. It was near here, at Hanwell, just 99 years ago (1835) that Brunel began to construct this railway. The Act authorising it, obtained after a titanic struggle, only received Royal assent on August 31st of that year, and the young and energetic engineer (he was then under thirty) actually started work hereabouts before the year was out.

To return to our locomotive : twice the distance of the axle pin from the axle centre is the travel or stroke of the

Motion of " King " Class Locomotive

piston, and this is obvious if you give it a little thought. In order to get four power impulses to a revolution, the pins or cranks of the right and left-hand engines of the two and-four cylinder locomotives are set ninety degrees apart.

The use of inside cylinders in the four cylinder locomotives renders it necessary to construct the axle of the leading driving wheels with cranks, as it is impossible to arrange for connecting rods to actuate crank pins attached to the wheels themselves, as is done when the cylinders are placed outside the frames. To counteract the effect of the moving parts (piston and rods, crank, etc.) on the running of the engine, balancing weights are placed on the coupled wheels and secured near the rims.

In the modern locomotive, two, three, four, and sometimes five pairs of wheels of the same diameter are connected by coupling rods, mounted upon pins secured to the outside of the wheels and forming the "rigid wheel base."

Steam is only admitted into the cylinders for a certain period of the piston stroke, depending upon the position of the valve gear, which actuates the valves from the movements of the driving axle and the crossheads.

After steam admission to the cylinder is cut off by the valve, the steam, by working expansively, continues to exert a gradually decreasing pressure on the piston until the valve reopens the port, this time to exhaust.

From the cylinders the exhaust steam passes through the blast pipe in the smoke-box and through the chimney to the atmosphere.

And I am glad we have got our steam off, for admittedly this is, and, I am afraid must be, just a little bit technical, but I hope you have been able to follow or, better still, keep up with it.

The 10.45 a.m. Train from Paddington

Near Hanwell, we pass the vast works of the Associated Equipment Company, makers of London's 'buses, and on through Southall, the junction for Brentford, we see factory after factory where well known brands of various household commodities are made. Here on the left at Hayes is the large creosoting yard of the Great Western Railway, where sleepers for carrying the rails are prepared, whilst on our right we pass the extensive " His Master's Voice " Gramophone Works. And so we speed onwards, through a thriving industrial area which reaches to West Drayton, where branch lines converge from Uxbridge and Staines. . . . Now we pass Iver, a station erected a few years ago to meet the needs of a new garden city.

"Up Main" meets "Down Relief"

Fox Photos.
We are Seven—"Kings" on Parade

"Castle," "King," and "Hall" Class Locomotives

HOW THE LOCOMOTIVE WORKS—(2)
CLASSIFICATION OF LOCOMOTIVES

ERE we might profitably return to our locomotive, I think. We have seen how the steam moves the engine after it gets into the cylinders, but what happens *before* that? Well, at the risk of being charged with putting the cart before the horse, we will now go back a bit.

Take a look at the steam chest (in this diagram) which is a chamber contained in the cylinder casting. The distribution of steam in Great Western Railway locomotives is made by using inside admission valves as indicated in the diagram. A piston valve consists of two pistons or valve-heads (see diagram) mounted on a single spindle, so as to control the passage of steam into and out of the cylinder.

On the regulator valve being opened by the driver from the footplate, steam is allowed to pass from the boiler, through the superheater (which is an appliance for heating the steam, after it has ceased to be in contact with water, above its generation temperature), to the steam chest between the valve heads.

You will see in the diagram that there are in the valve chest two cylindrical bushes, into which the valve heads fit and work, and between these bushes live steam enters from the steam chest, and on the outside exhaust steam passes from the cylinders to the blast pipe. In each of the

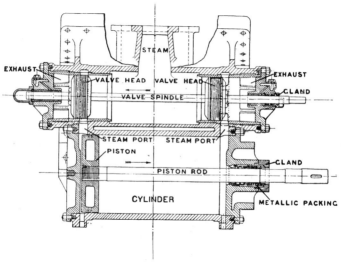

bushes is a port or opening leading to the corresponding end of the engine cylinder. Through these ports steam passes to and from the cylinder, entrance being possible only when the inside edge of the valve-head uncovers a port, and exit only when the outside edge of the valve-head uncovers the same port.

I think we have got that pretty clear, and now you will readily understand that when steam is admitted to the front end of the cylinder it will force the piston to the back end, and that when steam is admitted to the back end of the cylinder and the steam previously admitted to the front is allowed to escape, the piston will be forced forwards. And that, Sir, is how the reciprocating or " to-and-fro " motion is obtained at the cylinders which we have already turned into rotary motion at the wheels.

You noticed when watching the departure of the " Cornish Riviera Express " that the driver at starting partly opened his regulator. Steam is then admitted for about three-quarters of the whole period of the piston travel, but after starting the driver " notches up " his reversing lever, thereby restricting the travel of the valves, causing them to close the port earlier. This operation regulates the " cut-off," and after it, the steam in the cylinder works expansively. This period of steam admission or " cut-off " is varied by the driver according to the speed. At high speed engines are worked at " early-cut-off " and at low speeds " late-cut-off."

Yes, I was afraid you were going to ask about valve gears and I warn you that they are going to be a little difficult to explain, and frankly I think diagrams will tell you more than I can. The valve gears principally used on G.W.R. locomotives are Stephenson's link motion, Walschaërt's valve gear, and gears of its own design.

Here's a diagram of Stephenson's link motion and another of Walschaërt's valve gear. Shall I try and help you with the former, though it really wants a little more study that we can give it here ? You can keep the diagrams if you like, for by looking at them quietly at home, I think you will be able to understand them better.

Stephenson's link motion for one cylinder briefly consists of two eccentrics which, keyed to the axles of the driving wheels, act as cranks, the "throw" of which is about half the maximum travel of the valve. One of these eccentrics controls the forward, and the other the backward motion of the valve. Working around these eccentrics are "straps" to which rods forked at their forward extremities are attached, and between them, in

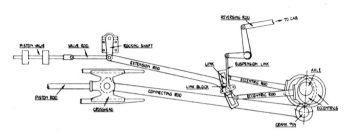

Diagram of "Stephenson" Valve Gear

the forks, is fitted a curved link, called the "expansion link." The "forward" eccentric rod is attached to the top and the "backward" rod to the bottom of the link.

You will see by the diagram that the link is supported by others, known as "suspension links," which are attached to a reversing shaft, an arm of which communicates, by means of a rod, with the reversing handle in the cab of the locomotive.

The expansion link can be either raised or lowered, effecting the reversing of the engine. It also governs the travel given to the valve, and thus varies the periods of admission and expansion of steam in the cylinders.

The extension rod which connects the valve to the link is forked at both ends, the rear enclosing both the link and also the block working in the slot of the link. The front end of the extension rod is attached to a " rocking shaft," and this in turn is connected, but outside the frames, to the valve spindle through a valve rod—all these parts being named in the diagram.

When the link is lowered as far as possible, the valve spindle is influenced by the " forward " eccentric, and in

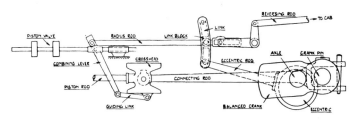

Diagram of " Walschaërt " Valve Gear

this position, known as " full fore gear," and when steam is admitted to the cylinders, the engine moves forward.

Contrariwise, when the link is raised, the effect of the " backward " eccentric is felt and the engine moves backward. This is known as " full back gear." " Mid-gear " is when the link is in the central position so that the eccentrics counteract one another's action.

Admitted that *is* rather involved, and as I warned you the mechanism is a little intricate for verbal explanation. But take courage, for I do not propose to say any more about Walschaërt's gear (though you can study the diagram) than that it is fitted to G.W.R. locomotives of the four-cylinder class on which it is arranged inside the frames, and to rail motors on which it is arranged outside the frames. On the G.W.R. four-cylinder engines two sets of valve gear are arranged to actuate all four cylinders, the outside cylinders being worked by means of rocking levers from the inside motion.

Just a word about lubrication. This is effected by feeding oil into the steam in the regulator box and steam pipes and it is carried in the form of a fine spray to the surfaces requiring lubrication. It is controlled by the regulator handle so that oil is only supplied when the engine is actually in motion. All other lubrication is by percolation of oil through an absorbent material from receptacles to the bearing surfaces. The oil cups are filled before the trip and during stops.

And now you have, I hope, at least a nodding acquaintance with the main principles of locomotive mechanism and you can ask me any questions you like, *except* " How does the railway locomotive work ? "

ဢ   ဢ   ဢ   ဢ

This is Slough, the junction for Windsor, where we stop for a few minutes. We get good views of Windsor Castle on the left just before entering and just after leaving the station. Slough has had a wonderful post-war development. It is the town of a hundred or more modern factories, and you see many of them from the train on the vast Slough Trading Estate, but notice that they are nearly all factories without chimneys, making little contribution to the smoke problem. They say industries are moving south. I do not really know if this is so or if new industries are selecting southern sites, but manufacturers are certainly

CLASSIFICATION OF LOCOMOTIVES

appreciating the fact that the Great Western Railway, with its extensive seaboard, proximity to coal fields, and fast freight train services, offers exceptional advantages to those placing their factories alongside its lines.

You see a hiking party is detraining here, and also a party of cyclists. They have taken advantage of the cheap fares offered to ramblers who can train to one station, hike across country, and entrain for home at another point. There are also cheap " self and bike " fares for cyclists, who can start their jaunts at places like this and so get right into the quiet and peaceful by-roads, cutting out the congested thoroughfares around London.

∽   ∽   ∽   ∽

Before leaving the locomotive you will want to know something about the different kinds of engines. There are three main classes—passenger, goods, and shunting—and these names are descriptive of their use. They may be sub-divided into :

Passenger : express, semi-express, stopping, suburban or branch trains.

Goods : fast vacuum fitted, ordinary goods and mineral trains.

Shunting : for work in goods yards and dock areas.

A passenger engine may on occasion be required to work a goods train ; a shunting engine, a local passenger train, and so forth. The need for a locomotive which will satisfactorily haul a passenger or goods train has led to the production of very useful " mixed traffic " type.

The nature of the traffic, the speed at which the train has to run, the weight of the load, and the character of the road (gradients, etc.) are all factors which have to be taken into consideration by the locomotive designer.

Wheel arrangement is a convenient way of classifying locomotives, and a simple one. It is based on the representation by numerals of the number and arrangement of the wheels of a locomotive from the front. For example, 4—4—2 denotes a ten-wheeled engine, the first figure being the number of wheels in front of the driving wheels, the second denoting the number of driving wheels, and the third figure indicating the number of wheels behind the drivers. In a ten-wheeled engine such as a " Castle " or " King " the arrangement is referred to as 4—6—o there being four wheels (bogie) in front, then six coupled drivers, and no other wheels behind the drivers.

Diagramatically the classes are represented by the wheels on one side only of the engine. This system of classification takes no account of the tender, but I ought to add that in the case of tank engines, that is locomotives without tenders, which carry their own water and fuel supplies, the letter " T " is added to the numeral indication.

The *G.W.R. Engine Book*, which you already have, will tell you how the names and numbers of the locomotives also run in classes such as the " Hall " Class (4—6—o)— Eaton Hall (4924), Hanbury Hall (4931), etc.; " Castle " Class (4—6—o)—Dudley Castle (4091) Dunster Castle (4093), etc.

There are also terms of American origin used for certain wheel arrangements but these are not so often heard now as formerly—" Pacific " (4—6—2), " Atlantic " (4—4—2), " Mogul " (2—6—o), " Consolidation " (2—8—o), and others.

CLASSIFICATION OF LOCOMOTIVES

Here are photographs of a few different types of G.W.R. locomotives, and you have a wider range in the album *Locomotives of the Great Western Railway.* You will see that the express passenger engines built for hauling heavy trains at high speed have six coupled wheels of large diameter. Coupling of wheels increases adhesion and that is why engines with a large number of coupled wheels, such as the 2—8—0 class, are used for heavy freight trains for, you see, nearly the whole weight of the engine is available for adhesion, being divided over the eight driving wheels. The smaller wheels give greater tractive force.

I really think that muſt be nearly all about the locomotive, if we are to talk about the permanent way, signalling, and other matters, but you can supplement my remarks by consulting the books I gave you.

I said *nearly all* about the locomotive, because I want to say juſt a word or two about how the engine takes up a supply of water from the track a little later on. So now shall we pass on to the railroad itself?

4700 Class Locomotive, Type 2—8—0

Laying Steel Sleepers

EN ROUTE TO SWINDON— TAPLOW TO READING

THE RAILWAY TRACK— STEEL SLEEPERS

E are now between Taplow and Maidenhead and about to cross River Thames and from Buckinghamshire to Berkshire, by a bridge which is unique in that it is the flattest arch ever constructed in brickwork —the work of the audacious Brunel, which was condemned by his contemporaries as unsafe nearly a century ago. It still stands and when the bridge had to be widened with the quadrupling of the track, the same design was followed, many years later.

Take a look out on the left from the bridge and you will get a glorious view of " Old Father Thames . . . rolling along down to the mighty sea." We shall see him three or four times more in our journey and cross his tracks again.

"CHELTENHAM FLYER"

Bridges bring us to the track known (quite wrongly, I think) as the "permanent way." With gigantic loco-motives, hauling trains of half-a-thousand tons at eighty miles an hour a sound track is absolutely essential.

You may know that when first laid down by Brunel, this Great Western Railway track was of broad gauge (7 ft. 0¼ ins.). Brunel was doubtless of opinion that higher speeds and bigger loads would be possible on his broad gauge. Many miles of railways of narrow (now known as standard) gauge had been laid down in various parts of the country, and when narrow and broad gauge came together trouble naturally resulted as all goods as well as passengers had to be transhipped.

What was known as the "Battle of the Gauges" was waged for some years, and whilst there is little doubt that the broad gauge had much to recommend it and many highly qualified engineers came forward to support Brunel's selection, in the end the narrow, or what is now the standard gauge (4 ft. 8½ ins.) won the day. Conversions from broad to mixed (broad and narrow) or standard gauges were made from 1858 onwards on the Great Western Railway, and the final conversion to standard gauge—a wonderful achievement of engineering—was carried out on May 21 and 22, 1892.

But why did they fix the gauge at such an odd measure-ment as 4 ft. 8½ ins.? Why not 5 ft. or 4 ft. 6 ins.? I think that 4 ft. 8½ ins. was possibly the gauge of early cart-road tracks which were converted to railways before the advent of steam traction, or perhaps the original rails were 3½ ins. on the face when a 5 ft. gauge measured from the centres of the rails would give 4 ft. 8½ ins. clear between rails —or perhaps like "Topsy," it just "growed" from what-ever happened to be the gauge of the first lines laid down.

Maidenhead Bridge

Typical
Section
of
Permanent
Way

"CHELTENHAM FLYER"

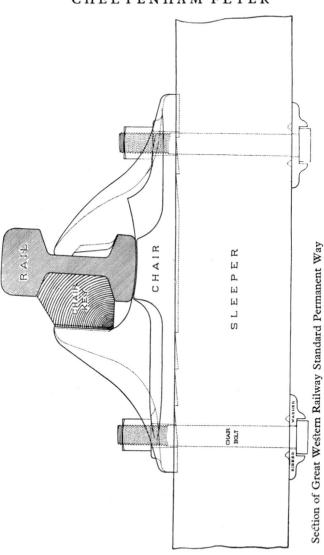

Section of Great Western Railway Standard Permanent Way

THE RAILWAY TRACK

The standard permanent way on this Railway consists of about twelve inches of " ballast," such as gravel or slag, which is placed upon the firm hard road (formation level). On the ballast rest the sleepers, which are creosoted timbers, 8 ft. 6 ins. long, 10 ins. broad, and 5 ins. deep. These are generally placed about 2 ft. 7 ins. apart and carry cast iron " chairs," which are $14\frac{1}{2}$ ins. by 8 ins. at base and 46 lbs. in weight. The chairs are secured to the sleepers by bolts and the rails are fixed in the chairs by means of wooden or steel blocks known as " keys," which are hammered in between the outer jaws of the chairs and the rails. The rails incline slightly towards one another. Standard main line rails weigh 95 lbs. to the lineal yard. The rails are 60 feet in length, and the ends are joined by means of " fish-plates " bolted to the rails.

You may have noticed that a small space is left between the ends of the rails, generally from a quarter to half an inch, and I know you will expect me to add that this space is left to allow for expansion due to heat, for I remember being so informed at school, as perhaps you were. But latterly engineers have been experimenting with the welding together of the ends of the rails into long lengths and, strange to say, no trouble has been experienced due to expansion or contraction ! That rather knocks the old theory on the head and it is almost unbelievable—but none the less true. It is, in fact, now found that spaces between rail ends need be no more for rails of 200 feet in length than is now allowed for the 60 feet rails !

The fish-plate is generally 18 ins. in length and has four bolts, two in the end of each rail, but a smaller 10-inch plate is now being extensively used having only two

69

bolts, which enables the sleepers to be brought closer together at the joint, so reducing the overhang of the rail.

You probably know better, but a celebrated author (who shall be nameless) makes the hero in one of his books see " the bright steel up-line . . . wedged in *fish plates* that were nailed to sleeper after sleeper." He was a bit mixed there, but great people do make mistakes and even Lord Tennyson in his " Locksley Hall," which is full of profound prophecy, wrote, when inspired by the (then) new experience of railway travel—

" Let the great world spin for ever
Down the ringing grooves of time."

and afterwards explained that he really thought the railway carriage wheels were grooved and not flanged. That, however, was in the very early days when railways were in their infancy.

But we must get back to our chairs and sleepers, and here is a sectional diagram which will explain more clearly than verbal description the various features of permanent way construction. On curves the outer rail is raised above the level of the inner to reduce friction caused by centrifugal force and to ensure stability of the trains when travelling at high speed.

Gradients or variations in the rail level are denoted by the number of lineal feet in which the line rises or falls one foot, and boards indicating the gradients are fixed at the side of the rails for the guidance of engine-drivers and others. You will not, however, see many gradient boards on this journey as the track is remarkably level ; in fact, the stretch of railway from London through Reading, Swindon and Bristol to Taunton—one of 160 miles—is the most level in the whole country, and that is largely due to Brunel who made cuttings or tunnels boring through hills, and threw up viaducts in the valleys to ensure a level road.

While we have been studying the permanent way, we have passed Maidenhead, the junction for the Wycombe Line, and are now approaching Twyford. Somewhere about here, on the " Up " Relief Line, a stretch of track is laid experimentally with steel sleepers. Look out on your right now and you will soon see it. . . . There it is.

Although British railways use about four million sleepers annually for relaying and new construction and twice that number of " chairs " to carry the rails, it may be that the familiar wooden sleepers with their cast iron chairs, will disappear in the course of years, to be replaced by steel.

Already about 190 miles of Great Western Railway track have been laid with steel sleepers. These are of various types, but by far the largest number have " cast on " chairs ; some have the chairs welded on to the sleepers, and in another type the jaws of the chairs are ingeniously formed by turning up a part of the sleeper plate.

The steel sleeper with " cast on " chairs consists of a steel plate pressed into the form of an inverted trough, the chairs (of cast iron) being cast on in such a way that the molten metal flows through slots in the plate and forms elongated " snugs," which securely fasten the chairs to the sleeper.

Yet another novel type, also under test in the track, is the " all in one " or " unit " sleeper, in which each sleeper and its two chairs are pressed out in one piece. This marks a further step towards the " all-steel " railway track, which promises to be the permanent way of the future. All these types of steel sleepers are in course of testing to see how they behave under traffic and what their lives are under varying conditions.

The special feature of the " unit " type is that the sleeper and chair for holding the rails are made integrally from a rolled steel plate, thereby avoiding the necessity for any fastening of the chair by bolts, welding or other means.

The steel plates from which the sleepers are made are 14 ins. wide and $\frac{7}{16}$ths inch thick, cut into 9 ft. 6 ins. lengths, and cold-pressed to form two waves near the ends of the plate, these waves eventually forming the chair. The plates are heated and passed through two hydraulic presses, and again, after re-heating, subjected to two more operations which finish shaping the sleeper section and finally " nose " the jaws of the " chairs " over to the correct angle and width. The sleepers are then carried by conveyor through a bath of tar mixture, to give them a protective coating, after which they are ready for use.

A particularly interesting feature of the chair is that, not only is the key side-tapered in the direction the wooden " keys " are driven, so that the farther the key is forced into the chair the tighter it becomes, but it is also undercut, or inclined towards the rail jaw, for the purpose of holding the rail firmly down on to the rail seat. The gauge, tilt of the rails, and the space between the jaws for the reception of rails and keys, are all automatically fixed during the operations of pressing.

Experiments are also being made with steel keys with

Unit Type Steel Sleeper

promising results and, if these and the steel sleeper are eventually found to be satisfactory, it will prove highly beneficial to the steel trade of this country, for whilst the timber for sleepers has to be imported—chiefly from the Baltic countries—steel sleepers are manufactured here.

Now that railway wagons and carriages are made very largely of steel—where wood was once used—it really looks as if the day of the all-steel railway is not so far off.

Take a look at this photograph of a " unit " type sleeper and you will see how ingeniously it is contrived out of one piece of metal.

Passing Twyford, the junction for Henley-on-Thames, world-famed for its annual Royal Regatta—we are soon in Sonning Cutting—a reminder that the permanent way of a railway involves cuttings, tunnels, bridges and viaducts. This is an excellent example of a railway cutting and of Brunel's way of going through a hill to keep his road level.

" As level and as straight as possible, and ' hang the expense ' " seems to have been the policy of this bold and unconventional young engineer. He evidently believed it was " better to go straight than move in the best circles," for the original intention was to avoid this hill by taking the line further to the right.

The largest tunnel on the Great Western Railway is that under the estuary of the Severn, and has a length of

Laying Steel Sleepers in Sonning Cutting

4 miles 628 yards. It is not only the longest railway tunnel in this country (excepting the Underground Railways) but the longest under-water railway tunnel in the world. It is 30 ft. below the deepest part of the river bed, and took 13 years to construct. A magnificent example of bridging is the Royal Albert Bridge over the estuary of the Tamar at Saltash—another of Brunel's masterpieces—whilst at Crumlin in South Wales there is a famous viaduct which comprises ten spans of 150 feet each with a total length of 500 yards and an extreme height of 190 ft. above rail level.

There is one feature of the railway track I have omitted, and that is the quarter-mile posts alongside the line, which you can see on your right particularly well here. These indicate the distance from Paddington and with the aid of a good stop watch it is quite easy to calculate the speed of a train in which you may be travelling. Keep that in mind and we will test the speed of " Cheltenham Flyer " this afternoon. This little table will help us, and you can keep it handy. As you see by counting the number of seconds between the quarter-mile posts, we get the speed in miles per hour. It is based on the fact that nine hundred, divided by the number of seconds occupied by a train travelling between any two quarter-mile posts, will give you the speed of the train in miles per hour.

Time in seconds between quarter-mile posts.	Speed of train—Miles per hour.	Time in seconds between quarter-mile posts.	Speed of train—Miles per hour.
10	90	21	42.8
11	81.81	22	40.9
12	75	23	39.11
13	69.2	24	37.5
14	64.28	25	36
15	60	26	34.6
16	56.2	27	33.3
17	52.9	28	32.1
18	50	29	31
19	47.4	30	30
20	45		

The railway track has to stand up to a pretty stiff test, and constant attention is necessary to ensure that degree of smooth running for which the Great Western Railway is famous. Before we leave the subject you may like to know something about the methods of keeping the track up to concert pitch.

The line is divided into lengths and each length is under the care of a gang of men, supervised by a ganger, who patrol it daily on the look out for any fault which may

Royal Albert Bridge, Saltash

develop, making minor adjuſtments as necessary. The gangs are aided in their work by modern equipment of various kinds, and where the mileage to be covered is extensive, as on single lines, motor trolleys are in use for moving men quickly along the lines whilſt the ganger has a motor inspeċtion car for his own use.

Portable arc welding plants are in use for building up worn crossings on the spot by adding metal to replace that loſt in wear and this work can be carried out between the passing of trains and without any interference with the traffic.

There are also appliances for deteċting any unevenness in the track, and one of the machines, similar in principle to a seismograph, or earthquake recorder, is placed on the floor of a coach such as this and, operated by a clock-work mechanism, automatically records on a winding drum any vibrations out of the ordinary, either vertical or lateral, so that the engineers can immediately locate the imperfeċtions.

THE RAILWAY TRACK—STEEL SLEEPERS

Another way of finding any " offending spots " is by means of a specially equipped vehicle which makes a whitewash " splash " for every irregularity exceeding a certain pre-determined degree met with, and every splash tells a story to the engineer. These methods of " feeling the railway bumps," play an important part in ensuring the high standard of smooth running which is attained, and it is this close attention to detail which enables passengers to read or write, dine or sleep, in perfect comfort when travelling at high speed.

As we emerge from Sonning Cutting, you see Messrs. Sutton's Seed Trial Grounds on your left, ablaze with flowers; you get another view of Father Thames on your right; and now you will have no doubt about where you are, for here are Messrs. Huntley & Palmer's extensive factories—for this is Reading, where the biscuits come from and where we make a short stop.

Crumlin Viaduct

The First G.W.R. Streamlined Rail Car

Fox Photos

RAILWAY TICKETS—STREAMLINED
RAIL CARS—SIGNALS

EADING is a rapidly growing town, and one reason for its progress is that it enjoys one of the best, if not the best, train service in the country. This accounts for its popularity as a business and residential centre. Though 36 miles from London, it has a frequent service of "non-stop" trains in both directions, which do the journey in forty minutes, little more time than is occupied in travelling to and from the outer suburbs of London.

ⲟⲟ   ⲟⲟ   ⲟⲟ   ⲟⲟ

Here's the collector for our tickets. I hope we can satisfy him. . . .

You have probably wondered, when taking a long railway journey, particularly if passing over the lines of more than one railway, why it was necessary for the collectors to punch pieces out of your ticket so frequently.

If you could follow that ticket after you have finally given it up, at the end of your journey, however, you would understand better why the ticket collectors had shown you so much attention, and if you were to examine your ticket carefully you would see that no two " bites " made by the collector's nippers were alike. These punches and impressions, of which some hundred different kinds are in use, tell the story of your travels to the initiated. It says to the person who ultimately examines it in the Audit Office of the railway, that you commenced your journey at A, changed at B to another railway, travelled *via* C to your destination at D, and the money you paid at the booking office for the ticket will eventually be divided between the railways concerned in proportion to the mileage you covered on each of their lines.

The ticket collector also assists passengers by ensuring that they are in the proper trains and carriages for their respective destinations, and by notifying them if, and where, any changes of train are necessary on their journeys. He also has other duties, for sometimes a young man (otherwise proud of his adult status) is apt temporarily to forget he has passed his fourteenth birthday and can no longer travel with a half-fare ticket. Then there are persons who omit to take any tickets at all, while others have a tendency to use first class carriages whilst holding third class tickets. The ticket collector is there to point out their respective lapses of memory, to rectify them, and generally to prevent irregularities or fraud of any kind. So be very careful.

RAILWAY TICKETS

In the earliest days of railways, the authority for a person to travel was a form filled in by the clerk at the station, who " booked " every person's journey, hence the terms " booking office " and " booking clerk," both survivals of the old coaching days as, of course, are the terms " driver," " guard," and " coach."

The small cardboard ticket now so familiar was the invention of a station master named Edmondson about 80 years ago, as also was the first ticket-dating and numbering machine. Railway tickets are still dated much in the same way, but they are now numbered in the process of printing.

Besides ordinary first and third class tickets for thousands of stations, there are many other varieties, as for example " summer," market, excursion, tourist tickets, day tickets, and a host of others. The tickets as supplied to the stations are numbered from 0000 to 9999, and are kept in numerical order in the " tubes " in the booking offices ; the lowest number being issued first in each case. The Great Western Railway does its own ticket printing, and in the year 1933 printed $50\frac{1}{2}$ millions of card tickets in 47 different colour combinations.

⌒   ⌒   ⌒   ⌒

Reading is an important railway junction. Here the direct line to the West of England leaves the old main line (*via* Didcot and Swindon to Bristol, which we are travelling) and proceeds *via* Newbury, Westbury, etc. It is also an important point of exchange with the Southern Railway.

But whilst we have been talking something of interest has arrived at the platform on your right. Take a good

Streamlined Rail Car No. 1

look at it, for it is the first streamlined rail car to be introduced. It is being tried experimentally on the service
between Southall, Slough, Reading and Didcot.

This car, which is so unlike any other railway vehicle
in the country, is the outcome of scientific tests made to
reduce wind resistance which, you may be surprised to
hear, requires more power to overcome than to propel the
car itself along the tracks. The effect of streamlining has
been to reduce wind resistance to about one-fifth of that
of a square-ended car.

The car, which weighs 20 tons and is 62 feet in length,
has been designed for a speed of 60 miles an hour. It
seats 39 passengers and is equipped with a 130 h.p. heavy
oil engine using non-inflammable fuel, and can be driven
from either end.

STREAMLINED RAIL CAR

As I have said, it is an experimental type and its performance will be watched with keen interest, but I may tell you that it has already been decided to extend the experiment, and cars similar in outward appearance are now being put into service on the Birmingham-Gloucester-Newport-Cardiff line. This innovation is primarily for business people, and the cars, which are equipped with

twin engines of 130 h.p., will cover the $117\frac{1}{2}$ miles between the Midland and Welsh capitals at an average speed of $56\frac{1}{2}$ miles an hour including stops. They are actually designed for maximum speeds of 75 to 78 m.p.h.

These new cars are luxuriously appointed, being heavily carpeted, and the seats for the 40 passengers being arranged in pairs on each side of a central gangway. Removable tables are provided for meals or business purposes, and each seat has soft lighting from the back—just above the shoulder level. Hot and cold water are provided in the lavatory, and there is a cafeteria and bar. These new streamlined cars are, in fact, luxury expresses, but ordinary third class fares are charged with a supplement of half-a-crown only per passenger.

What was that? Oh, the crest at each end of the car. It is that of the Great Western Railway, and consists of an amalgamation of portions of those of the Cities of London and Bristol, and embodies their mottoes. The crest dates from the incorporation of the Company in 1835 and the original scheme was for a railway from Bristol to London —hence the design. The newer cars bear the familiar standard G.W.R. monogram in place of the crest.

ᔕ   ᔕ   ᔕ   ᔕ

We are off again, and as we leave Reading, you see on your right the high ground of Caversham Heights, at the foot of which is one of the finest reaches of the Thames.

At Reading are situated the signal works of the Great Western Railway, and that seems to give us the cue for a talk about signalling. Having got our locomotives (with their trains) on the move on our perfect track, we must ensure means of controlling them and that is the purpose of signals.

ᔕ   ᔕ   ᔕ   ᔕ

You know, of course, that the road for a train—that is, the route it is to travel—is " made " by the signalman by the movement of points or switches. I mention this because I was once travelling through a busy junction by fast train when an (otherwise) enlightened fellow passenger, who

84

Chassis of Express Streamlined Rail Car

had been gazing out on the line, remarked that in his opinion the public did not appreciate the responsibility the engine drivers had in *steering* their trains over the proper track, particularly at night with only coloured lights to guide them !

Well, you knew better than that, but it just shows how little some people know, or how little they can really think about such things, doesn't it ? A great thinker and writer has said : " It is unwise to assume that anyone knows any-thing," but I'm afraid we shall not get far if we work on any such assumption to-day.

Although colour light signals which, as we saw, are installed between Paddington and Southall, are rapidly coming into use, the railways are generally signalled by means of the familiar semaphore type of signal which gives two positions, " danger " being indicated by the arm in its normal position, at right-angles to the post, and " all right " by the arm being lowered to an angle of about 45 degrees.

As you can see for yourself, the signal posts on the Great Western Railway are generally placed on the left-hand side of the line as viewed by the driver on the engine footplate. The signal arms are on the left side of the signal posts and all *stop* signals are painted red with a white stripe, as seen by the engine driver, and white with black stripe on the reverse side. The distant signals (caution only) are amber with a black stripe on the obverse, and white with black stripe, like the stop signals, on the reverse.

Attached to the signal posts are cases containing lamps, which on the Great Western Railway, are burning

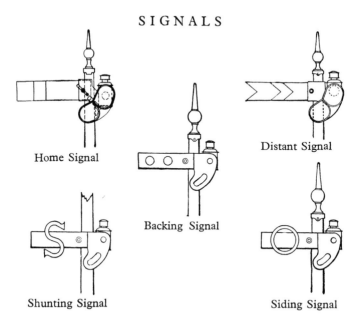

Home Signal

Distant Signal

Backing Signal

Shunting Signal

Siding Signal

continuously day and night, except when being trimmed and cleaned. A special form of lamp, economical in oil consumption, is used, which requires trimming and filling with oil about once a week only. To the signal arms are attached coloured spectacles through which the lights of the lamps are viewed by the oncoming engine drivers. When the arm of a " ſtop " or " diſtant " is in the " all right " or " off " position, a green light is seen, and when in the " danger " or " on " position, a red light shows in the case of a " ſtop " signal and an amber light in the case of a " diſtant " signal. There is a small white back-light which shows in the opposite direction as an indication to the signalman that a signal arm is working and that the lamp is burning.

"CHELTENHAM FLYER"

You know, of course, that the movements of trains along the lines are controlled by signalmen in signal boxes, the signals being worked by levers and suitable connections. Electrical instruments are provided for the use of signalmen in communicating with the signal boxes on either side. These signal boxes are so placed along the line of railway, as to divide it up into lengths, which are known as block sections protected by signals and (note this particularly) the normal position of all signals is at " danger."

The distant signal is a caution signal only and the only caution signal. The " caution " position of the distant signal corresponds to the " danger " position of the stop signal. The distant is the first signal to be reached by a train approaching a signal box, and is distinguished from all other signals by its arm being fish-tailed. It gives information to a driver as to the state of the line ahead, and it is the only signal which can be passed by a train when the arm is in the horizontal (" caution ") position. It is fixed at such a distance from the next signal ahead that when it is at " caution " a driver has sufficient time to bring his train under control in order to stop on reaching the home signal (i.e., about a thousand yards on a falling gradient, eight hundred yards on the level, and six hundred yards on a rising gradient). When the distant signal is at " all right " the driver knows that he can continue to run at his usual speed, and that he will find all the other signals for the section controlled by the distant signal also in the " all right " position.

At terminal stations and at places where a speed restriction is imposed, such as on curves, the distant signal is permanently fixed in the " caution " position to warn the driver to be ready to reduce speed or pull-up.

The amber light is, of course, to render the distant signals distinctive from the stop signals by night, just as the fish-tails do by day.

The home signal is the second signal reached and is usually near a signal box. It is a stop signal and must not be passed at " danger." Its function when " on " is to stop a train clear of any junctions there may be with other lines, and also clear of the next section ahead.

The starting signal is the third signal reached, and is placed in such a position that any shunting or other operations which may have to be performed at the signal box can be carried out without having to pass this signal, which controls the entrance of a train into the next section ahead. In some cases an advance starting signal is provided about a train's length or so ahead of the starting signal, *e.g.*, when there is a cross-over road or other points ahead of the starting signal.

The home, starting, and advanced starting signals are all stop signals, and these (with the distants) are the " running " signals of an ordinary section of railway. There are, of course, several other signals which are used for different purposes, such as shunting, backing, etc., and each has its distinguishing indications. Here are illustrations of some of them which you can keep by you.

And just here, with your kind sanction, I should like to take a short " breather." Sidney Smith, you know, once said of Macaulay that he " has occasional flashes of silence that make his conversation perfectly delightful." So——.

"Cheltenham Flyer" picking up water

"Times" Photo

LOCOMOTIVE WATER TROUGHS — HOW SIGNALS CONTROL TRAINS

DURING our discourse we have passed Pangbourne, and are now approaching Goring and Streatley Station near which are the Goring water troughs, and you will remember I promised to say a word or two about the locomotive picking up water from the track. Well, now is our opportunity, for here are the troughs between each of the four pairs of rails. You will notice the peculiar rumble of the train as we are passing over them. On the right you also see the water-softening plant—the water having to be treated so as to remove the salts which would cause " fur " or scale in the locomotive boilers.

All modern tender locomotives are fitted with water scoops for taking up water at speed. The hinged scoop, something like a shovel, is fitted below the tender and controlled from the footplate. It normally lies close up against the bottom of the tender, and when lowered by the fireman when running over the troughs, the scoop takes off the top layer of water and the speed of the train forces it up through an internal pipe to the tank. The end of this pipe is above the ordinary water level of the tank, and over it is fitted a sort of inverted dish to deflect the water into the tank, where of course it is trapped, the displaced air escaping through vents. A float indicator on the tender records the amount of water in the tank, and the fireman watching this indicator raises the scoop accordingly. You may be surprised to know that from two to three thousand gallons of water are picked up in this way in about a quarter of a minute, provided the speed

of the train is fifty to sixty miles an hour. A long drink, but a quick one.

Lying between the rails, the troughs, which contain the water, are of galvanised steel plate, 18 ins. wide and 6 ins. deep and extend for about a quarter of a mile. Water trough installations are generally 50 to 60 miles apart. The troughs are kept filled from storage tanks to which supplies are pumped, and the water level of the troughs is controlled by a ball valve on the same principle as the household cistern.

Tapper Bell

The first experiments on the Great Western Railway for taking water supplies at speed from the track were made at about this spot in 1895. Without these water troughs long " non-stop " train runs would, of course, be impossible.

Sorry for butting in on our signalling talk, but I thought it would be more interesting to tell you about the water troughs where you could see them for yourself.

꙳꙳꙳ ꙳꙳꙳ ꙳꙳꙳ ꙳꙳꙳

To revert to our signalling. As I have said, a signalman can communicate by means of electrical instruments with the signal boxes on either side of him. He also has a telephone at his disposal.

Perhaps the best way of explaining how a train is passed forward is to assume we have three signal boxes along the line, which we will call Red, White and Blue, in the order named. Now each signal box has a tapper-bell for each section on either side for both " up " and " down " lines, and by means of a code, messages are sent and received on these tapper bells regarding all trains passing through these sections. One beat on the bell calls attention. This signal is given before any other bell signal. On receipt of this signal the signalman immediately acknowledges it by repeating it.

Key Disc

Let us now imagine then that we have a train travelling from Red's section through White's, to Blue's.

When White receives the bell signal " Is line clear ? " from Red, he has to satisfy himself that there is no train in his section and that the line is clear for a distance of a quarter of a mile (the " clearing point ") inside his home signal. If this is the case, White repeats the bell signal to Red's signal box and brings into use his (White's) key-

93

disc instrument. Now, this instrument has three positions, "Line clear," "Line closed" (normal), and "Train on line." When a train can be accepted from Red's signal box, White, after sending the bell signal, pegs the key-disc instrument in his signal box to show "Line clear," and his action simultaneously records "Line clear" in a keyless disc instrument in Red's signal box. You will observe that the disc instrument in the box in the rear, being keyless, is under the control of the signalman in the box in advance. That is important, as we shall see.

Permission is thus given for the train to be sent forward, and Red, after lowering his starting signal for the train to proceed, at once sends another bell signal to White's signal box, "Train entering section." Upon receipt of

Keyless Disc

this, White alters his key-disc instrument from "Line clear" by pegging "Train on line," and again in so doing a similar indication is simultaneously shown in the *keyless* disc instrument in Red's box. White then, in turn, offers the train to Blue's box, in exactly the same way as Red offered it to White and if Blue's section is clear up to the clearing point, Blue gives "Line clear" to White, pegging his key-disc accordingly and so gives the "Line clear" indication in White's *keyless* disc.

In that way, the sequence of operations between Red's and White's signal boxes is repeated between White's and Blue's signal boxes, and so on in each pair of signal boxes, as the train proceeds.

HOW SIGNALS CONTROL TRAINS

When the train arrives at White's box and is found to be complete (*i.e.*, carrying a red " tail lamp "—illuminated at night—on the laſt vehicle) White, when he has replaced his diſtant, home, and ſtarting signals to " danger," sends a bell code signal to Red " Train out of section," and unpegs his key-disc inſtrument from " Train on line," which then shows the normal indication which means " Line closed."

Similar operations are gone through for trains on both " Up " and " Down " lines, and I think you can already see how they ensure that only one train can be in one section on the same line at one time.

When sections are very short—as in the case of junctions —the " Is line clear " signal is passed forward as soon as it has been acknowledged to the signal box in the rear. When the next signal box in advance is within a quarter of a mile of the home signal in rear, the signalman in advance muſt not give " Line clear " to the signal box in rear until " Train out of section " for the previous train has been received from the next signal box ahead.

It is obvious that on busy sections of line, where the diſtance between signal boxes is short, a faſt train would be slowing down every minute or two whilſt " Line clear " was being obtained. To meet cases of this kind, the " Train approach " signal is used, and it enables several sections to be cleared ahead so as to ensure a clear line, and every time a certain signal box is reached in a chain of boxes, the signalman ſtarts the " Train approach " signal, so that a further length of line is prepared for the passage of the train. Here is an example of what I mean. A to D are a firſt group, E to J a second group, and K to P a third. " Line clear " has been obtained from signal

95

INTERIOR OF G.W.R. SIGNAL CABIN

boxes A to D and when the train reaches C the " Train approach " signal is passed to E, who in turn starts " Line clear " for another chain of signal boxes stopping at J. At H the " Train approach " signal is given, and so on.

That, then, is briefly—and I wish I could have been more brief—the normal procedure in passing a train on its journey on an ordinary double line track, where no obstruction exists.

You may wonder how the signalman knows the character of the train that is approaching him. The class of the train is indicated by a code of bell signals. There is also a special series of engine headlights in use which indicates, by the arrangement of the lamps, the class of the train.

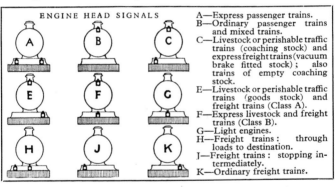

ENGINE HEAD SIGNALS

A—Express passenger trains.
B—Ordinary passenger trains and mixed trains.
C—Livestock or perishable traffic trains (coaching stock) and express freight trains (vacuum brake fitted stock) ; also trains of empty coaching stock.
E—Livestock or perishable traffic trains (goods stock) and freight trains (Class A).
F—Express livestock and freight trains (Class B).
G—Light engines.
H—Freight trains : through loads to destination.
J—Freight trains : stopping intermediately.
K—Ordinary freight trains.

And here we are passing Cholsey and Moulsford Station, which is the junction for the old-world river-side town of Wallingford.

Further help is afforded in the working of the heavy Summer passenger traffic on Saturdays on the Great Western Railway, by large three-figure numbers displayed in a slotted frame on the smoke-box doors of locomotives

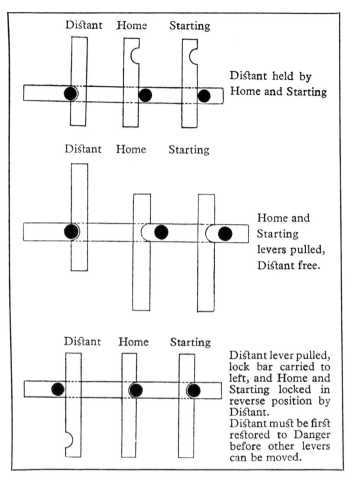

Distant   Home   Starting

Distant held by
Home and Starting

Distant   Home   Starting

Home and
Starting
levers pulled,
Distant free.

Distant   Home   Starting

Distant lever pulled,
lock bar carried to
left, and Home and
Starting locked in
reverse position by
Distant.
Distant must be first
restored to Danger
before other levers
can be moved.

of the West of England express trains.   These numbers can
be identified a quarter of a mile away when approaching,
and tell the signalmen or station staff the time of the train,
its starting point, its destination, and whether it is running
in two, three, four or five parts.

Locking Frame of Signal Box

EN ROUTE TO SWINDON—CHOLSEY TO DIDCOT
SIGNAL BOX EQUIPMENT—INTER-
LOCKING—TRACK CIRCUITING

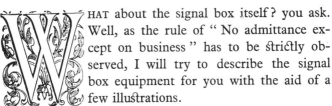

HAT about the signal box itself? you ask. Well, as the rule of " No admittance except on business " has to be strictly observed, I will try to describe the signal box equipment for you with the aid of a few illustrations.

What would strike you first on entering a signal box would be an array of large levers alongside one another in a frame. Some of these levers are connected with the various signals by wires and others with points, etc., by iron rodding. The levers are painted in distinctive colours to assist the signalman in his work—distant signal levers are yellow, " stop " signal levers are red, point levers are black, facing-point lock levers blue, detonator-laying levers white with black band, while any spare levers are painted all white.

In order to operate the signals, points, etc., the levers are pulled forward or pushed backward in the frame.

The backward position, by the way, is the normal one in all cases, and when levers are in the backward position, the signals are at danger and points set for the main line. The levers are held in position backward or forward by a catch which is released by pressing a spring handle when moving a lever.

The tapper bells, key and keyless discs and telephone instruments for communicating with adjoining boxes are on a shelf at a convenient height above the levers, and a " locking diagram " showing the arrangements in the section is placed in full view of the signalman when facing his levers and instruments.

Here is a photograph of the interior of a manually operated signal box showing the levers, each of which bears on its face a plate with a large number at the top, while in some cases there are small numbers below. The top numbers refer to the signals, points, etc., as numbered in the locking diagram (seen in front of the signalman), and where small numbers appear these refer to the " leads," that is, any other levers which, owing to the interlocking of signals, etc., have to be moved before the lever can be released.

As you probably know, " points," or " switches " as they are sometimes called, are the means by which trains travel from one pair of rails to another. They consist of pairs of movable hinged rails, tapering at their points, inside fixed rails, and are worked from the signal box by iron rodding supported on roller bearings. The hinged end of the points is referred to as the " heel " and the thin blade-like end, the " toe." When the " toe " faces a train in the running direction the points are called " facing

Interior of electrically-operated Signal Box

points," and when the train passes over the " heel " first they are known as " trailing points."

Well, I think that is all about points for the moment, except to say that compensators are provided which counteract any expansion or contraction of the iron rodding, and that in some cases ground or " disc " signals are provided at points.

And that brings us to the subject of interlocking, a fascinating one in itself, although we have not time to go very fully into it this morning. Interlocking means that the levers obstruct or free the movements of one another in such a way as to ensure safe and correct working of points and signals, and to prevent the exhibition of con-flicting signals.

From what I have already said, you will, I am sure, be able to appreciate the necessity for the signals being so interlocked that the distant signals cannot be lowered until

Exterior of modern G.W.R. Signal Box

after the home and starting signals have been lowered. The " home " and " starting " signals are, therefore, " leads " for the distant signals. In a similar way any points connected with the running lines must be in correct position for the passage of a train before the home or starting signals can be lowered, and this is secured by interlocking between signals and points.

Each lever is provided with a " tappet " or " tail piece," which is attached to it and moves backward and forward with the lever. Running at right angles to this tappet, and close to it, either under or above, are the lock bars. These bars in the smaller frames are provided with studs or wedge-shaped pieces, fitted in such a manner as to impede the movement of the tappets when the levers to which the tappets are attached should be locked.

The interlocking mechanism is below the signal box floor level and, in a large signal box, is a very complicated looking affair, but like most complicated problems, interlocking is simplified when you take it stage by stage, and I think with the diagrams I have given you, you will be able to follow it in principle quite easily. These three simple little diagrams represent the locking and back-locking which takes place between the distant, home, and starting signals, at, say, quite a small roadside station, and the methods here described are repeated *ad infinitum* with the locking of all points and signals in the locking frame.

Whilst discussing signal box equipment, I ought perhaps to add that signalmen are assisted in their duties by numerous appliances designed with a view to safe working. One of the most important of these is, perhaps, what is known as " track circuiting," which is installed when special circumstances require this additional protection.

A length of railway line is insulated to form a complete electrical circuit by having insulated fishplates on the rail joints at each end. The rails between these insulated fishplates are joined together by wire bonds to enable the electric current to be continuous. The electric current is provided by means of a battery fixed at one end, and the current is made to pass through a mechanism called a " relay " at the opposite end of the length of line track circuited. In the signal box is provided an indicator which shows " track clear " when no train is on the track circuited portion of line, and is immediately altered to " track occupied " as soon as a train enters upon the track circuit. By these means a signalman is able to tell when his line is " clear " or " occupied " by a train, even although the train on the line is entirely out of sight. It is also possible for the lever working the signal leading on to the track circuited portion of line to be electrically locked, so as to prevent an " all right " signal being given when the line is not clear.

Electric " repeaters " are provided in signal boxes for signals which are not visible from the signal box, in order

Interior of Electric Power Signal Box, Paddington (Arrival)

that the signalman may know when the levers operating
the signals have done their work. The signal arm itself
is repeated by a miniature flag in the signal box instrument
showing " on " or " off," and the signal lamp by a flag
showing " in " or " out." In the case of a lamp failing
and the flag showing " out," a bell is made to ring in
order to attract the signalman's attention.

COLOUR LIGHT SIGNALS

Before leaving the subject of signalling you will like to hear something of the latest developments in colour light signals and electric power signal installations.

As already pointed out, the four passenger lines between Paddington and Southall have been equipped with colour light signals and the semaphore signals removed. The type of signal used is known as the searchlight. It throws a powerful beam of light easily " picked up " from the engine footplate.

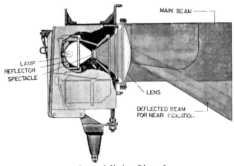

MAIN BEAM

LAMP
REFLECTOR
SPECTACLE

LENS

DEFLECTED BEAM
FOR NEAR INDICATION.

Searchlight Signal

The indications given by the semaphore signals have been reproduced light for light in the new colour light signals, so that the same indication is now given by day and night, instead of, as formerly, by the semaphore by day and by lights at night.

Here is a diagram of the searchlight signal which you can study at will. As you see it consists of a multi-colour spectacle, much like, but much smaller than a semaphore signal spectacle. This miniature spectacle moves in front of a concentrated filament lamp combined with a special optical mirror.

The large black disc around each colour light signal is to provide a suitable background for the light beam. The beam is also protected from the direct rays of the sun by a hood projecting forward from the black disc.

Normally a red (stop signal) or yellow (distant signal) light is projected through a clear lens in front of the spectacle, the light being changed to green as the spectacle is moved by operating an electrical control, when the signal lever is reversed. The spectacle falls by gravity to give a red or yellow light when the signal lever is put back to its normal position.

There being no mechanical wires between signal box and signals, the necessary detection of points is effected electrically. Repeaters are provided in the signal box to shew whether or not the lamps are burning and to shew the position of the spectacles, *i.e.*, red, yellow or green.

A distant colour light signal can only shew a green light when its relative home and starting signals are shewing green lights.

I ought to add that the four lines are continuously track circuited, the track circuits being used to replace the signals to danger and to lock the levers controlling the signals. Starting signals are locked in their " normal " position until " line clear " is received from the signal box in advance, and any signal replaced to danger by the operation of a track circuit cannot again shew a green light till the controlling lever has been put back to normal and pulled again.

Three power-operated signal boxes have been provided at Paddington in connection with the new works there. Electric power signalling installations with colour light

Colour Light Signal Gantry

signals have also been installed at the new stations at Cardiff and Bristol.

Any attempt at a technical description of the equipment or working of these boxes would take us quite out of our depth I am afraid, but you will get some idea of the equipment from these photographs. You will particularly note the miniature " levers," and how they contrast with those in a manually operated signal box. The interlocking is accomplished electrically in one of the boxes at Paddington (Westbourne Bridge) and at the Paddington Arrival and Departure Boxes mechanical interlocking is used.

Illuminated " spot-light " diagrams of the lines and signals are provided in front of the signalmen and two small red lights for each track circuit, the lamps lighting when the track circuits are occupied.

You see you are already getting some idea of the provisions made to ensure the control and safety of the trains along the track. That is by no means the whole tale of safeguards, but we must break off a while now, as we are running into Didcot Station.

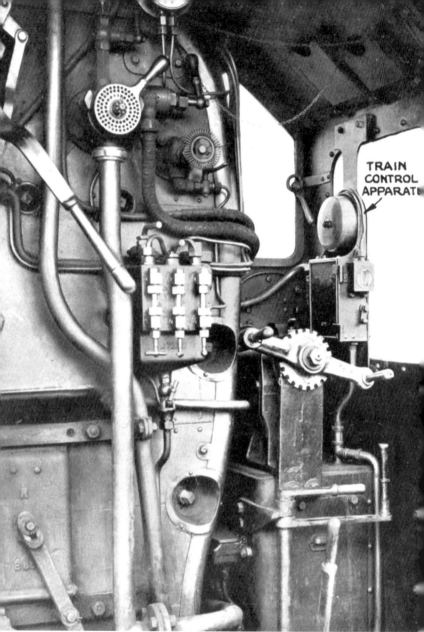

TRAIN
CONTROL
APPARATU

Automatic Train Control Apparatus—Locomotive Cab Equipment

AUTOMATIC TRAIN CONTROL—SAFETY APPLIANCES—FOG PRECAUTIONS

IDCOT Station has recently been considerably enlarged. It is an important railway junction, for from here a line runs northward *via* Oxford to Aynho Junction, where it joins the direct line from London to Birmingham and the North, while another line goes off southward to Newbury and Winchester.

We have a six minutes stop here, and just about time for a short chat on automatic train control, and some of the many other devices for ensuring the safety of trains.

The Great Western Railway has been a pioneer in the matter of automatic train control combined with audible locomotive cab signals, and 376 track miles have been installed with the equipment for over a quarter of a century.

"CHELTENHAM FLYER"

It was recently decided to extend the equipment to no less than 2,130 miles of main line, as shown on this sketch map, and this formidable task has now been completed, involving the fitting of the necessary equipment to 1,320 signals and 2,000 locomotives.

This system gives audible signals to the engine driver in the cab of the locomotive, corresponding to the position of the distant signals. When the distant signal is at the " all right " (off) position a bell rings, and when the distant signal is at " caution " (on) a siren sounds and at the same time the brakes are automatically applied. The application of the brakes and the sounding of the siren continues until the engine driver " acknowledges " the signal by lifting a small handle on the apparatus in the engine cab.

You can appreciate the value to the engine driver of the audible signals in his cab at any time, but particularly when the murky mantle of " King Fog " (the railways' greatest enemy) descends and blots out the landscape, including the fixed signals alongside the line.

The apparatus on the permanent way consists of an immovable ramp between the running lines at or near each distant signal. The ramp consists of a baulk of timber about 40 ft. long, on which an inverted tee bar is mounted, the highest point being 3½ ins. above the rail level. To the ramp is connected an electric battery, the circuit from which is closed and opened by a switch coupled to the lever in the signal box operating the signal. This switch is closed—thus energising the ramp—when the signal is in the " clear " position : and is open—thus leaving the ramp electrically " dead "—when the signal is in the " caution " position.

AUTOMATIC TRAIN CONTROL

The equipment on the locomotive comprises an electric battery connected to an electro-magnet, which controls a valve in the vacuum brake system. The circuit from this engine battery is closed and opened by a switch which is operated by a shoe, or plunger, fixed on the centre line of the engine.

The plunger projects to within $2\frac{1}{2}$ ins. of the rail level, and is consequently lifted one inch each time the engine passes over a ramp. When the engine is not on a ramp, the switch is closed and the electro-magnet is energised, keeping the brake valve shut. When the engine passes over a " dead " ramp—the signal being then in the " caution " position—the plunger lifts, opens the switch, and breaks the circuit. The electro-magnet is thus de-energised, and allows the brake-valve to open, admitting air to the brake pipe through a siren, and applying the brakes.

When the engine passes over a " live " ramp—the signal being at " all right " (off)—the circuit on the engine is broken, as before, by the movement of the shoe, but the current from the ramp is picked up by the plunger, and flows through the electro-magnet, thus keeping the brake-valve shut, and also causing relays to work and to ring a bell on the engine.

I should add that the automatic train control ramps provided in connection with colour light signals are incapable of being energised to give a " clear " indication in the cab of the engine, unless the distant signal is showing a green light and the lever controlling the distant signal is in the reverse position.

You see, the engine driver gets a distinctive audible signal in his cab at every distant signal, whatever the

Automatic Train Control Apparatus—shoe in contact with ramp

position of the arm may be, so that the apparatus gives him a " location " indication under all conditions. The mechanism, I may add, is adaptable to double or single lines of railway.

∽ ∽ ∽ ∽

I mentioned " facing points " in connection with signal box equipment and you can appreciate that these would be a source of danger if not in alignment for passing trains, but this is assured by the provision of facing point locks and locking bars at all facing points on passenger lines.

Here is a photograph of a facing point lock, which consists of a " stretcher blade " joining the two switch blades and pierced with two holes. A plunger, worked by a separate lever in the signal box, passes through one of the holes in the stretcher blade according to the direction in which the facing points are set, and prevents any movement of the points until the plunger is withdrawn.

The facing point lock lever is interlocked with the home signal, and the latter cannot be lowered until the facing point lock lever has been operated. In order to make security even more secure, another appliance is brought into use, viz., the locking bar.

Even the possibility of the signalman inadvertently withdrawing the plunger whilst the train is actually passing over the point has been provided against, and a bar, sufficiently long to cover the wheel-base of the longest vehicle in use, is fixed inside the rail just to the rear of the facing points. It operates on a series of cranks in such a manner that when moved it rises and falls, and when rising would be stopped by the flanges of any wheels passing over the points at the time.

Facing point lock

The locking bar is worked by the same lever as the facing point lock, so you can see that it is quite impossible for the signalman to unbolt the points when a train is passing over them.

But nothing is left undone that can be done in this matter of safety and, in regard to facing points, there is still an additional safeguard provided in the form of a detector lock, which serves to detect anything wrong with the points in the event of the facing point lock failing to act, and also to prevent signals governing such points being lowered until the points are in correct position.

In the event of such remote contingencies as the rodding which connects the facing point lock with the signal box either breaking or being out of adjustment, the stretcher blade breaking, or the points being run through in the trailing direction and damaged, the fact would be discovered by the detector lock.

The main idea of the detector lock is that a blade or some similar device, worked in connection with the points, shall cross the path of another blade or blades worked in connection with the stop signal or signal protecting the points in such a way that, if points are in any respect out of adjustment, the blade working off the points will obstruct the pulling of the signal wire.

Among other safety appliances of note are " fouling bars " which are provided where the fouling point between converging tracks cannot clearly be seen from the signal box, and there is any risk of a signalman giving permission for a movement along one track which is partly obstructed by a vehicle standing on another.

Fouling bars are similar in form to, and are the same length as, facing point locking bars, and are fixed with one end at the actual fouling point. When any vehicle is foul, the bar cannot be moved, and thus it prevents a train approaching on the obstructed line.

You will remember we mentioned detonator-laying levers in the signal box. Well, at certain signal boxes, detonator " placer " machines are provided, worked by a lever from the box, by means of which the signalman is able to place two detonators on the rail in advance of the home signal for use when the fixed signals are obscured by fog, etc., or in any other emergency in which it is necessary for the signalman to stop a train. When the detonator " placer " lever is in the normal or forward position, *i.e.*, away from the signalman, the detonators are under cover

Detonator placed on rail

in an iron casing fixed close to the rail and slightly below rail level, and when the lever in the box is reversed, the detonators are thrust forward upon the rail head.

You may have heard the explosion of a detonator, but perhaps you have not seen one ; it consists of an explosive contained in a round metal case and is used to give an audible signal (a bang) to the driver of a train in fog, falling snow, or when the fixed signals cannot be clearly seen. When placed by hand on the rails, detonators are secured by lead strips and exploded by the wheels of an engine passing over them. To be certain of a report two are placed in position and an ingenious apparatus known as a " detonator economiser " uses the impact of the first to remove the second detonator, so if the first one " goes off " the second one is recovered intact.

During fog, or falling snow, the arrangements for signalling are considerably tightened up, the speed of trains reduced, and every precaution taken to ensure a train being stopped short of any obstruction. The fogmen report for duty and are stationed at distant signals to place detonators on the lines when the signals are in the " caution " (on) position. For this purpose detonator-placing machines are largely in use to prevent the fogman crossing the lines. In addition to placing detonators the fogmen exhibit red hand signals to oncoming engine drivers.

When the distant signal is at " all right " (off) the fogmen remove the detonators from the rails and show green hand signals to engine drivers. The absence of a hand signal after a detonator has exploded must, according to the regulations, be regarded as a " danger " signal.

You will now appreciate, I am sure, that in passing trains along the line all other precautions are subservient to that of safety, and I ought to add that in the event of any failure of any part of the mechanism the signals would go to the danger position. A simple example of this is the signal arms which are so weighted that if the signal wire should break the arms, if " all right " (off), would come back to the " danger " (on) position.

You see the railways are taking no risks with the safety of their passengers.

Single Line Setting-down Post

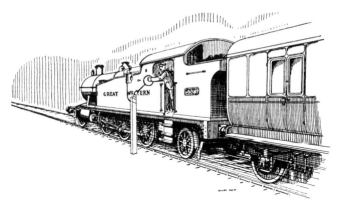

CHAPTER THE TWELFTH

EN ROUTE TO SWINDON — DIDCOT TO
WANTAGE ROAD

SINGLE LINES OF RAILWAY —
COACHING STOCK

I SEE our guard is anxiously consulting his watch and apparently we are all ready to proceed, but are waiting for our scheduled departure time. Time-keeping is an important matter on the railway, and the Great Western Railway prides itself on the punctuality of its trains both in the matter of departure and arrival times.

In the very early days of railways, and before the coming of telegraph communication, the matter of time-keeping was not so easy. In those days different towns kept different times according to their longitude—" sun " time as it was called. For example, Reading time was then four minutes later than London, and Penzance was twenty minutes later and still is, of course, in the matter of " sun " time, which is why those glorious west coast resorts get daylight so much longer in the evenings now Greenwich time is generally used.

The railways had, of course, to maintain a standard time. London time was adopted at all stations and in the country was known as " railway time." This naturally created some difficulties, but with the coming of the telegraph matters were simplified for the railways, as Greenwich time could be communicated from London.

The maintenance of standard time is of vital importance on the railway to-day, as you can well imagine. How do you think Greenwich mean time by which all the clocks and watches are set is notified to the 1,500 stations on the Great Western Railway ? Well, it is done in this way : on the very tick of ten o'clock the time is sent out from Paddington Station each morning and comes from Greenwich, when all telegraph lines are kept open for the purpose, as the " time " signal takes precedence over all other business.

At 9.58 a.m. the Post Office tape machine in the Telegraph Office at Paddington gives a warning message— " Time, Time, Time " and on the stroke of ten o'clock comes the time signal—" Ten, Ten, Ten." When the warning is received all telegraph clerks stand by, having suspended other operations, in readiness to flash the time signal simultaneously throughout the line.

As I think I told you, the " Up " Cornish Riviera Express leaves Penzance at 10.0 a.m. daily, and the train is actually despatched by the telegraphed time signal. A horn is sounded at the station as the time signal is received and this gives the guard the signal to pass the " right-

Single Line Picking-up Post

away " to the engine driver. So that is a pretty accurately timed start.

Whilst on the subject of time-keeping, you may like to know that for all the revenue earning trains on the Great Western Railway, for the year 1933—and there were no fewer than 1,647,475—the average number of minutes late was only 2.4. When you think of what fog and adverse weather generally can account for, as well as necessary checks during reconstruction work, etc., that is a pretty good time-keeping record ; don't you think so ?

" Cheltenham Flyer," by the way, is the best timekeeper on the whole of the Great Western Railway system—and that is saying a good deal ; in fact, it is not putting it one whit too high to say that the " Flyer " gives the time to the countryside through which it passes every afternoon on its trip from Swindon to London.

There goes the guard's whistle and we are off now on the final part of our journey, for there is no further stop till we reach Swindon.

Soon after leaving Didcot Station we pass on our right the Store Depôts of the Army and Royal Air Force, which extend for some miles.

As I said just now, a line goes off from Didcot to Newbury and Winchester. This is a single line of railway, and perhaps we might devote a few moments of our time to the working of such single lines, for our remarks up to the present have been confined to double-lined (up and down) track. Where one line of railway serves trains in both directions it will be apparent that different arrangements have to be made for ensuring the safety of the trains.

A feature of single line working is that the engine driver shall have in his possession some visible evidence of the permission given him by the signalman to bring his train upon a section of single line, and the various forms of single line working " train staff," " train staff and ticket " and electric " staff," " tablet " or " token " are all based on this common principle.

SINGLE LINES OF RAILWAY

The simplest form of single-line working is the train staff system, and it applies to short branch lines worked by one engine in steam. The train staff is about the length of, and not unlike, a policeman's truncheon, and bears upon it the names of the stations at either end. With only one engine in operation, there is obviously no possibility of collision and the staff is simply a visible authority to be upon the line.

To enable a staff to be picked up and set down without stopping a train, a loop is provided at the end of the staff, through which the fireman places his arm in picking up. The loop is placed over a horn or hook at the setting down post, as shown in these photographs.

But you will ask me what happens when it is necessary for two or more trains to proceed in one direction where there is no intermediate service in the opposite direction, so that after the passage of the first train the train staff is not brought back to the signal box from which it was issued for use by the second train? Well, that is where the " ticket " arrangement comes in, and there is a regulation that no train is permitted to leave a signal box unless the driver is either in possession of, or actually sees the " staff." Where a second train is to follow in the same direction, the driver of the *first* train is shown the " staff " and handed what is known as a " train staff ticket." The tickets, which are kept in a special box at the signal box, cannot be taken out without the

Electric Train
Staff Instrument

train ſtaff, as the key of the box is affixed to the end of the ſtaff. Further, the key cannot be withdrawn unless the box has been locked, so you see a ticket cannot possibly be issued without the ſtaff. The train ſtaff and tickets for each section of the line are of a diſtinctive pattern.

The electric ſtaff, electric tablet, and electric token syſtems are all similar in principle, and one or the other is in use where a number of trains may have to run in one direction without an intermediate train in the opposite direction. Inſtruments containing the ſtaffs, tablets, or token are provided for each section of the line.

The combined action of the signalmen at each end of a section is necessary to release a ſtaff, tablet, or token, and only one ſtaff, tablet, or token can be out at a time for any section, so that when, say, a ſtaff has been taken out of an inſtrument and given to an engine driver at "A" who is proceeding to "B," a second ſtaff cannot be taken out at "A" until the firſt has been replaced in the inſtrument at "B," and then only by combined action of the two signalmen concerned.

The electrical mechanism which enables this to be done is quite simple, but I think you will already see how the safeguards work.

༄   ༄   ༄   ༄

We have passed Steventon and are getting rapidly along towards our deſtination, and though we have already been able to cover several railway subjects, so far we have said little about rolling ſtock other than locomotives. That is because carriages and wagons are so varied in size and design, and for that matter in purpose that I think, perhaps, a selection of photographs of different types of vehicles

G.W.R. Special Saloon " Queen Mary "

would be more helpful than a lot of talk about them. So you can look through these at your leisure and remember that you will have an opportunity of seeing something of carriage and wagon construction at Swindon, where all the Great Western Railway rolling stock is built.

You have seen the modern coaching stock provided on the " Cornish Riviera Express " and at this moment you are having evidence of the comfort of a G.W.R. carriage, and I think you'll agree that it leaves little to be desired.

You may, however, be interested in some special saloon cars built by the Great Western Railway for the rapidly increasing traffic in Ocean passengers on its Plymouth-London route. The wise counsel contained in the slogans " Land at Plymouth and save a day " and " Sail from Plymouth and save a day " has induced ever-increasing numbers of ocean passengers to take the four hours' scenic route of the Great Western Railway between Plymouth and London and *vice versa*. It is for their comfort and convenience that these special cars, which approach the

Interior of Special Saloon

ultimate in rail travel comfort, have been conſtructed and put into service.

These cars, which are the firſt of their kind to be built by a British railway, embody many novel features and refinements, and exemplify what is lateſt and beſt in railway car conſtruction.

By the gracious permission of His Majeſty King George V, each of the eight cars is named after a member of the Royal Family—" King George," " Queen Mary," " Prince of Wales," " Duke of York," " Duke of Glouceſter," " Duchess of York," " Princess Mary " and " Princess Elizabeth."

COACHING STOCK

The car bodies are 60 ft. long and 9 ft. 7 ins. wide like those of the Cornish Riviera Express—the widest in the country. Each car is divided by sliding doors into two sections seating seventeen and eight passengers respectively, and there is also a coupé compartment seating four. Large armchairs are provided for seating at small tables. The cars are in polished walnut veneer with exquisite figured burr walnut panels. Overhead lighting is achieved by means of concealed electric lights covered by satin glass panels flush with the stippled vellum ceilings. In fact, these cars are a real triumph of British craftsmanship and a pleasing achievement in colour harmony.

We have it on no less authority than Sir James Barrie that " You can't be b'aith grand and comfortable," and whilst not quite clear, perhaps as to his precise meaning, I am pretty certain our best beloved of writers had not experienced a journey in one of the G.W.R. luxury coaches *before* he penned those words.

∽　　∽　　∽　　∽

There's Wantage Road, the station for the town of Wantage. The old steam tramway which connected station and town for half a century (1875-1925) was the first steam tramway to be used by the public in the British Isles. Wantage, as every schoolboy knows, is the birthplace of Alfred the Great. I don't know if boys still read " Tom Brown's School Days," but if you are acquainted with that classic, you may be interested to know that what is referred to as the " Blowing Stone of King Alfred " can still be seen, and " blown," nearby.

The man who pulled the communication cord of the " Cheltenham Flyer "
By H. M. Bateman

VACUUM BRAKE — EMERGENCY
SIGNAL — SLIP COACHES

N ow let us see if we can follow the working of the vacuum brake. You probably know that the effect of pulling the emergency chain, which you see above you, is partially to apply the vacuum brake.

You have, no doubt, heard some of the yarns told about passengers pulling the emergency chain and the fine for doing this without just cause, and while some of them may be true, the majority are, I am afraid, fictitious. I expect, however, you will like Mr. H. M. Bateman's picture of the passenger who pulled the emergency chain in " Cheltenham Flyer." Here it is, as it appeared in the *Tatler*.

The emergency signal is, as I have said, one adaptation of the vacuum brake, so let's have a look at the brake equipment and try and follow how it works. You know what a vacuum is, of course, but if asked you would not, I hope, reply like the schoolboy who said " I have it in my head but can't express it." Now such a thing as a perfect vacuum is not obtainable, and we have to be

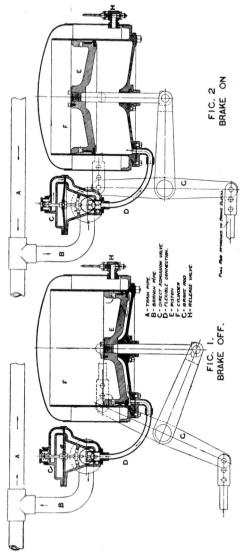

A - TRAIN PIPE.
B - BRANCH PIPE.
C - DIRECT ADMISSION VALVE.
D - FLEXIBLE CONNECTION.
E - PISTON.
F - CYLINDER.
G - BRAKE ROD.
H - RELEASE VALVE.

FIG. 1.
BRAKE OFF.

FIG. 2
BRAKE ON

Pull Rod attached to Brake Blocks.

Vacuum Brake Apparatus

content with a partial vacuum, which, to all intents and purposes, is what is meant when the word vacuum is used.

The railway automatic vacuum brake consists of a continuous vacuum pipe, which extends under the coaches, throughout the train and from which, under ordinary conditions, air is withdrawn by an air-exhausting device on the engine ; and a brake cylinder and vacuum reservoir combined under each coach of a train.

If you will take this diagram you will, I think, be able to follow what I have to say. It illustrates the position of the cylinder and vacuum chamber when the brake is off (on the left) and on (on the right).

Brake cylinders are fixed under each passenger vehicle, and on long coaches such as that in which we are travelling, two cylinders are provided. The piston is surrounded by a rubber flap which allows the air to be drawn from, but *not* to return to, the upper portion of the cylinder and surrounding reservoir. As you see, the cylinder is connected by a branch pipe to the train pipe which extends underneath each vehicle. On small vehicles, with one cylinder only, the connection with the train pipe is made direct, whilst on large vehicles like this with two cylinders the connection is made through the medium of a " direct admission " valve, which is clearly shown in the diagram. The train pipe connects with adjoining vehicles by flexible hosepipes which rest on airtight stops when not in use.

The vacuum is created by means of an ejector on the engine which exhausts the air from the train pipe and cylinders. Whilst running, the required vacuum is maintained by an air pump on the engine, and gauges are provided both on the engine and in the guard's van, which register the amount of vacuum created.

The brake is applied by the engine driver opening a valve on the engine, or by the guard opening the cock in his van, and admitting air rapidly or slowly at will.

When the brake is applied, air flows into the train pipe, and raises the diaphragm of the " direct admission " valve. The air from the atmosphere is thus admitted through the top valve and flows to the lower portion of the cylinder in sufficient quantity to reduce the vacuum to the same amount as in the train pipe. The pressure of the air in the cylinder has the effect of raising the piston, and by this means actuates the brake rods by which the brake blocks are applied to the wheels of the coach.

The brake is released either by the engine driver re-creating the vacuum, or by the release valves of the cylinder being opened and so admitting air to the upper side of the piston and equalising the pressure.

The main features of the vacuum brake may be briefly summarised as follows :

1. It is continuous in its action.
2. It can be applied over the whole length of the train and engine at the same time.
3. It can be worked upon trains of any length without difficulty.
4. It can be applied either by the engine driver, the guard, or a passenger.
5. It is automatically operated on both portions in the event of a train parting.

With regard to the last point, you will readily understand that in the event of any severance of the flexible hosepipes the vacuum would be destroyed and the brake applied.

As I have already said, the effect of pulling the emergency chain is partially to apply the vacuum brake, and as a certain amount of vacuum is lost, the fact is at once shown on the vacuum gauges on the engine and in the guard's van. Further, two small discs are exhibited (one in each side) at the end of the coach in which the chain is pulled, and when pulled, the chain remains slack and cannot be replaced by the passenger. So you see the

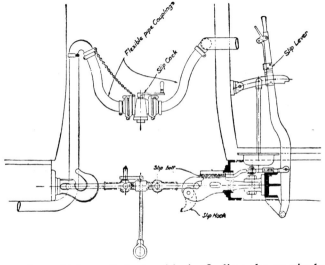

guard would have little trouble in finding the particular compartment.

The engine driver, on feeling a partial application of the vacuum brake and seeing the indication on the vacuum gauge fixed on the engine, would at once infer that the emergency chain had been pulled and bring his train to a stand as soon as possible.

In addition to the automatic vacuum brake, hand brakes are provided on the engine and in the guard's van of passenger trains, for use in the remote event of any failure of the vacuum brake mechanism.

∽   ∽   ∽   ∽

The vacuum brake leads us to slip coach working, for one of the problems that puzzles a good many, and may puzzle you, is why when the slip coach is cut off and the brake pipes severed, the coach and the main train are not both brought to a stand.

We saw this morning that the " slip " coaches for Westbury on the Cornish Riviera Express were placed in the rear of the train, and the slipping apparatus between the " slip " and the main train was coupled up as shown in this photograph, and here is also a diagram which will help you to follow the operation of " slipping."

This is performed by means of a lever (which I pointed out to you this morning) by a slip guard who rides, as we saw, in the front vehicle of the section slipped, the apparatus being fixed in his compartment. The release hook of the " slip " is hinged on a pin and retained in its normal position by means of a sliding bar coupled up at one end to the lever, the other end of which rests and bears on the hinged portion of the hook. The lever has three positions—" main train," the running position, " slip and brake on," and " release," and is connected to and controls a large three-way plug cock situated in the vacuum brake system, containing ports connecting to the train pipe, brake cylinder, reservoir, and the atmosphere. A non-return valve is fitted between this cock and the reservoir.

Between the vacuum brake couplings are fitted two adaptors, secured to them by pins and lugs, the bodies of

Guard releasing Slip Coach

which, when together, form a coupling capable of being pulled apart with no damage to either. Contained in the adaptor fitted to the coupling of the main train portion is a small valve, which, when closed, seals the train pipe. This valve is held open when the gear is coupled by a cross-member in the adjacent adaptor fitted to the "slip" portion, and when the gear is disconnected automatically closes.

The screw coupling and flexible connections of the vacuum system are prevented from falling away after the " slip " has been made by chains. Collapsible brackets and chains are used on the steam-heating connections, holding them in position.

So much for the apparatus. Now let's see what actually happens when a slip is detached. On nearing the place where the " slip " is to be made, the driver, if necessary, slightly reduces speed, and the guard of the " slip " pulls the lever right back to the " slip and brake on " position. This causes the sliding bar to come away from the drop portion of the release hook, permitting it to fall and, leaving the shackle of the screw coupling free to fall also, thus disconnecting the draw-bars and causing the slip portion immediately to fall away from the main portion of the train.

The vacuum brake and train-heating connections are pulled apart, the main train portion of the former, and both portions of the latter, automatically sealing. With the lever in this position, the three-way cock is admitting air to the brake cylinder, so applying the brake on the slip portion. Speed is thus reduced slightly and, the train portion having proceeded, the guard places the lever in the " middle " or " release " position, connection between the atmosphere and the brake cylinder is closed, and

Main Train dropping Slip Coaches

connection between the brake cylinder and large reservoir established. Air rushing from the former to the latter releases the brake. The guard can then apply or release the brake at will until the vacuum in the reservoirs is destroyed. The capacity of these reservoirs is such that at least three separate applications of the brake can be made.

Having exhausted the vacuum, the guard cannot restore it, and consequently skill and judgment are needful in order to bring the " slip " to a stand at the required position at the station. An independent hand-screw control of the brake gear is, however, provided, enabling the guard to apply the brakes gradually without using the " vacuum " portion of the gear, thus reserving his vacuum for the final application.

A small slipping signal is fixed at the point at which the guard has to operate the slipping mechanism in order to bring the slip portion of the train to a stand at the station platform. To enable the slip guard to give warning of approach to any persons on the permanent way, a bell actuated by a foot bellows is fitted in his van.

There is a special arrangement of tail lamps on slip coaches to signify to signalmen when one or more slip portions are carried on a train.

Steam-heating (lower) connection between Coaches

TRAIN LIGHTING AND HEATING

UR talk on the vacuum brake and slip-coach working has brought us through Challow and the station we are now approaching is Uffington.

It is connected by a short line with the old market town of Farringdon, the service being maintained by a small branch train. It must have been here, I think, that the story of the pompous overseas visitor and " Cheltenham Flyer " originated, but of course, I cannot vouch for it.

Please stop me if you have heard it.

Whilst waiting one afternoon at Uffington Station (shall we say ?) to meet a friend, the gentleman in question got into conversation with some of the railway staff on the

platform, to whom he held forth on the vast superiority of everything in his own country, the railways in particular, where it appeared the engines were finer and the trains considerably faster than in this " lil' old country " of ours. It was in the midst of his flow of superlatives that, with a shrill whistle and roar, " Cheltenham Flyer " rushed through the station and was gone in a flash. . . . .
" Gosh ! " exclaimed the man from the land of big things as he recovered his breath, " what*ever* was that ? " . . .
At which one of the porters, without raising his eyes from the job he was doing, remarked laconically : " That'd be our branch train shunting, stranger."

Now look over the Downs on your left and you will see the famous Uffington White Horse, the oldest of our " White Horses," which marks the site of the battle of Ashdown in 871. To commemorate his victory over the Danes, King Alfred's soldiers cut out the white horse—a badge or symbol of Hengist (stone horse)—on the hillside by removing the turf and exposing the chalk subsoil. Rather a queer looking steed, isn't he ? But he's well over a thousand years old, remember. By the way, the ancient Icknield Way runs along the crest of these Downs.

     ꙾   ꙾   ꙾   ꙾

If you are as curious as I am about railway matters, you will probably want to know how continuous electric lighting is provided in steam trains, for it is available whether they are going forwards, backwards, fast, slow or standing still.

On electrified railways the lighting of the coaches is, of course, a comparatively simple matter, as the current is available for driving and heating the train, and it can equally well be utilised for illumination.

142

TRAIN LIGHTING AND HEATING

On electric railways the " shoes " or collectors in contact with the conductor rail or overhead wires collect the electricity and the cables connected with the shoes distribute the current throughout the train for any or all of the purposes required. With few exceptions, however, the railway lines connecting cities and towns in this country are constructed for steam traction, when the problem is not so simple, and other means have to be found to provide electricity for train lighting.

In the early days, trains were lighted by means of oil lamps. Then came the flat flame gas-burner using compressed oil gas. This was followed by the inverted incandescent gas-burners, an excellent illuminant, but with some disadvantages. As you see, the coach in which we are now travelling is fitted for electric lighting, and for many years past all new carriages constructed by the Great Western Railway have been electrically lighted. I am sure you are anxious to know how this is done.

You know, of course, that supplies of electric current for lighting our streets and homes are produced at large power stations, and you may have visited one of these stations and seen the mammoth steam engines and dynamos employed for the purpose of generating the current and the appliances used for controlling the supply in order to make it suitable for the many purposes to which it is put.

The electric current for lighting the railway carriage comes from a small power station situated underneath each coach. There is a dynamo for generating the electricity, a battery or accumulator for storing it, and a " regulator "—a very ingenious little appliance—which keeps the supply of current constant whatever may be the speed of the train. There is also an automatic "cut in" and "cut out" switch, which switches the dynamo off when the train ſtops, so that the current which has been ſtored in the battery does not run to waſte.

The dynamo consiſts of magnets with a rotary centre, known as the "armature," and this has to be turned round quite faſt in order to generate the electricity—familiarly known as the "juice" by electricians. This is done by means of a belt and pulleys, there being a large pulley on

G.W.R. Standard Electric Train Lighting Components

| A—Storage Battery. | C—Through Control Couplers |
| B—Dynamo. | D—Auto. Switch. |

the neareſt wheel axle, connected by a belt with the small pulley on the dynamo armature, which is made to turn three times as faſt as the wheels of the carriage. You know, of course, that a railway coach axle revolves with the wheels.

The battery is getting charged moſt of the time the train is in motion. While the train is running at or about twenty-five miles per hour the dynamo generates electricity at a proper pressure for the lamps and battery, but as the train slows down the pressure drops, and the automatic switch disconnects the dynamo from the lamps and battery. Until the train is again running at twenty-five miles per hour the battery alone takes up the work of supplying electric current for lighting the coach. The battery may be regarded as a tank into which the dynamo pumps all the electric current—generated and not being used by the lamps. From this battery the lamps can draw a supply of current when the train is stationary or running at low speed.

E—Regulator.   G—On and Off Switch.
F—Distant Switch   H—Fuse Board.

To charge the battery fully, the pressure across the terminals of the dynamo must be raised to thirty-three volts and, as this is higher than the lamps can stand, the regulator—a sort of little robot switch-board attendant—while taking care that the battery gets all the pressure it wants, sees that the extra pressure which would be injurious to the lamps is cut off and the charging of the battery automatically stopped when it has been loaded to capacity.

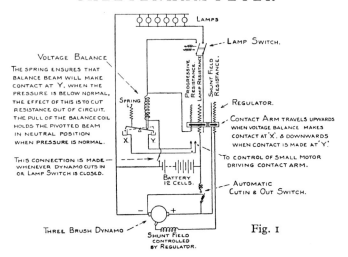

LAMPS

LAMP SWITCH.

VOLTAGE BALANCE
THE SPRING ENSURES THAT
BALANCE BEAM WILL MAKE
CONTACT AT Y, WHEN THE
PRESSURE IS BELOW NORMAL,
THE EFFECT OF THIS IS TO CUT
RESISTANCE OUT OF CIRCUIT.
THE PULL OF THE BALANCE COIL
HOLDS THE PIVOTTED BEAM
IN NEUTRAL POSITION
WHEN PRESSURE IS NORMAL.

PROGRESSIVE RESISTANCE LAMP RESISTANCE

SHUNT FIELD RESISTANCE.

SPRING

REGULATOR.

CONTACT ARM TRAVELS UPWARDS
WHEN VOLTAGE BALANCE MAKES
CONTACT AT 'X', & DOWNWARDS
WHEN CONTACT IS MADE AT 'Y.'

THIS CONNECTION IS MADE
WHENEVER DYNAMO CUTS IN
OR LAMP SWITCH IS CLOSED.

X   Y

TO CONTROL OF SMALL MOTOR
DRIVING CONTACT ARM.

BATTERY
12 CELLS.

AUTOMATIC
CUT IN & OUT SWITCH.

THREE BRUSH DYNAMO

SHUNT FIELD
CONTROLLED
BY REGULATOR.

Fig. 1

A distant switch is provided and enables the lights for the whole train to be turned on or off from any coach in the train or for the lights for a single coach to be switched on or off from the coach itself.

Here is a photograph showing the underframe of a coach and the electric lighting apparatus in position. You see the dynamo on the right in its metal casing, and the regulator enclosed in a box (side removed) with the automatic switch and fuse board.

This other photograph shows the various components of G.W.R. standard electric train lighting equipment.

I think that explains pretty clearly how the electric train lighting equipment works, but as I understand every schoolboy of to-day studies wireless circuits, you will doubtless be interested in these two diagrams showing

146

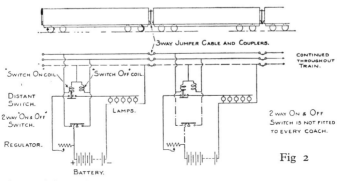

Fig 2

(Fig. 1) how the lamp voltage is kept constant at 22 volts with a maximum variation of plus or minus $2\frac{1}{2}$ per cent. and (Fig. 2) how the guard can switch the lamps "on" and "off" throughout the train, either from his own compartment or elsewhere.

You will, I think, agree that our small travelling generating station is rather a wonderful piece of mechanism. The dynamo is capable of working automatically equally well whichever way it is revolving, and of standing speeds up to ninety miles per hour, which means over two thousand revolutions per minute for the dynamo shaft, and while doing all this it is liable to sudden and violent shower baths from the locomotive when picking up water at speed form the troughs, and is sometimes away from a repair shop for many weeks at a stretch. You will readily understand that in all these respects it is at a disadvantage compared with the large power stations from which we draw our domestic supplies. Despite all this it does its job of work remarkably well and failures of the delicate and largely automatic mechanism are, considering all things, few and far between.

Steam-heating (lower) connection between Coaches

TRAIN LIGHTING AND HEATING

So much then for train lighting; but trains in winter muſt be warm as well as light and, although we don't require the heat to-day, perhaps we ought to have juſt a few words on how the coaches are heated.

This is accomplished by passing live ſteam from the locomotive boiler—at a reduced pressure of course—through a pipe syſtem running the length of the train to radiators situated under the seats in every compartment. Take a look under the seats here, and you will see them ; that metal guard is to prevent suit-cases and such-like being placed too close to the radiators.

The heating syſtem is composed of a ſteel pipe situated under the floor of each vehicle, at the ends of which are fitted flexible hose couplings similar, though smaller, to those used on the vacuum brake syſtem.

The supply of ſteam from the boiler is admitted to the train by the driver and can be further controlled, according to climatic conditions and the requirements of passengers, by the guard.

The driver's control consiſts of a ſteam-reducing valve, which is fitted into the cab of the engine. The aćtion of this valve reduces the ſteam pressure and maintains an even supply. The guard's control consiſts of a valve fitted in his compartment. When the pressure in the syſtem exceeds sixty pounds per square inch, a check valve fitted to the rear of the engine automatically opens, releasing ſteam to the atmosphere.

Heating is controlled in the compartments by means of the handle which you see under the luggage rack. When that heating syſtem is working, the handle, when placed in the " cold " position, closes the valve and prevents ſteam from entering the radiator, and when in the " hot " position, admits ſteam to the radiator.

PADDINGTON GOODS STATION

FREIGHT SERVICES — MAILS —
NEWSPAPER TRAINS

ELL, we have covered a good bit of ground this morning and I hope you have got something out of all this talk.

I should like to have told you the way in which the time-table is arranged, to have said something about all the preliminary work—the fitting in of a thousand details—which is involved in altering the time of an existing train or in putting a new one into the time-table.

Then if time had permitted we might have had a word or two about how the goods trains are marshalled and controlled, and there are many other subjects full of interest on which we have not touched. Perhaps, however, enough is as good as a feast, even if the diet is railways. Anyway, much must be left unsaid for we are passing Shrivenham Station and the next one is Swindon, where we alight.

You may be surprised to hear that freight services are, from a revenue point of view, more important to the railways than passenger services. It is the mineral and mer-

chandise trains on this railway that earn the larger part of
the income.

So far we have said little about the freight services of
the railway, but we depend upon them for our very existence. I wonder if you realise that nearly all your food,
clothing, fuel, letters and papers, practically everything
you eat, wear, or use comes to you by railway, but if you
only give it a little thought, you will see that it is so.

It has been truthfully said that "transportation is
civilisation." The conveyance of merchandise — raw
materials, food, clothing, fuel and the thousand and one
needs of this age—is a vital factor in human existence.

Try and visualise the activities of a large modern goods
station. From early morning motor lorries and horse-
drawn vehicles are taking out for delivery to shops, warehouses, factories, etc., a vast and varied assortment of
merchandise which has been sent off from stations all over
the country the previous evening. During the day, and
more intensively during the late afternoon, these motors
and horses bring in thousands and thousands of articles
of all sizes and descriptions, from truck loads to small
packages, for dispatch to destinations throughout the
whole of the country and for shipment abroad. All these
goods are sorted and loaded within a few hours of being
received and sent on their various ways in fast goods trains.

The Great Western Railway has about 90,000 merchandise wagons of various types and several hundred
booked freight trains run over its lines daily. A large
number of the latter are composed of vacuum-brake-fitted
stock, and travel at express speed between the larger towns,
whence branch connections serve outlying areas and give

Insulated
Meat
Container

20-ton
Mineral
Wagon

a " next morning " delivery, though the destinations may be some hundreds of miles from the starting point.

G.W.R. stations have goods depôts, sidings, and warehouses with up-to-date mechanical equipment for handling all classes of merchandise. Rail transport is supplemented by door-to-door collection and delivery by a stud of nearly 2,000 horses and well over 5,000 road vehicles, including a fleet of fast motor lorries.

Features of modern goods transport afforded by the Great Western Railway are express freight trains, " registered transits," railhead distribution, country lorry services and road-rail containers.

Most of the freight trains travel during the hours of darkness and less is, therefore, known of this side of the railway's activities. But these " trains that pass in the night " not only do so at express speed, but some of them make quite long " non-stop " runs.

The " registered transit " scheme is a sort of registered post arrangement for consignments of goods which are specially looked after along the journey with a view to delivery at destination at a specified time. Such consignments are marked with a green arrow which ensures urgent attention all along the route.

Railhead distribution is a scheme rapidly coming into favour with manufacturers, by which goods are forwarded in " bulk " to a railhead—such as Cardiff—and distributed from there by fast motor lorries to numerous towns and villages within a defined radius of 20 to 30 miles.

Country lorry services are particularly useful to farmers and the like, the motor lorries acting as feeders to the railway and distributors of goods arriving by railway.

A Household Removal by G.W.R. Container

These lorries have regular rounds and work to time-tables from over 150 centres on the Great Western Railway.

The use of road-rail containers is increasing daily, not only by manufacturers who send their goods in bulk and so save the cost of separate packing and casing, but for many other purposes, and particularly for household removals, for which they are admirably suited.

Household removals are typical of the " complete service " offered by the railway. The G.W.R. will estimate for the door to door conveyance of your household effects, including the services of packing and unpacking by experts.

A road-rail container, identical to a furniture lift van, is brought to the door from which the " move " is being made. The furniture is packed in it by experienced

These Little Pigs " Go Great Western "

packers, conveyed to the station, transferred to the rail and carried to destination by express freight train. On arrival the container is delivered to the new residence, the furniture unloaded and placed in position, and if required, carpets laid, pictures hung, and the whole transaction insured at low rates. But that is not all; the family removing get substantial reduction on their own rail fares to the new home. That is just another example of service offered by the Great Western Railway to-day.

You may not know that railways are, in law, " common carriers "—they cannot pick and choose their freights, but, with few exceptions, have to carry whatever is offered, and are fully equipped to do so. In the matter of transport, they are indeed universal providers, and the Great Western Railway is always happy to quote for the conveyance of anything from a school boy complete with tuck-box to a circus and menagerie including the " bigtop "—" caravans," artistes, animals caged and otherwise, and all the other paraphernalia. Whilst the G.W.R. carries some thousands of boys every term—the G.W.R. is a great schools line—it is also equipped to take the circus job and has done so on several occasions, whilst complete farms—personnel, animals and implements—are not infrequently taken " lock, stock and barrel " by special trains from old quarters to new, involving journeys of hundreds of miles. In short, " Send it Great Western " is just as sound as the excellent and familiar advice " Go Great Western."

Improved freight services mean a more rapid distribution of raw materials and manufactured goods, which is in every way advantageous to the traders and trade of the country. Whereas in the old days it was the practice for distributors to hold large stocks of goods, such stocks are now largely a thing of the past. The trader who orders his supplies by telephone or telegraph one day, can, relying upon fast freight train services, get delivery the following day, even though the goods have to be conveyed hundreds of miles. This means money in the traders' pockets, as less capital is locked up in stock and less storage accommodation has to be provided than was formerly the case.

Time will not, I am afraid, permit of our considering the many types of vehicles used for goods transport, for their name is legion, but here are photographs of a few, including a crocodile truck with a carrying capacity of 120 tons.

What *is* a crocodile ? Yes, perhaps as a railway term " crocodile " does need a little explanation. It is a name given to a class of long and low well trucks which are used for conveying large and heavy pieces of machinery and

Circus Elephants travel in " Pythons "

other consignments which would foul the loading gauge if carried on ordinary wagons.

" Crocodile " is the telegraphic code word for that particular type of vehicle. In order to economise in words and prevent any confusion when ordering or referring to particular types of wagons, a telegraphic code is in use in which zoological names are largely employed, and as is not unnatural, the various vehicles become known by these code names.

Some of them certainly seem more appropriate than others, and while " crocodile " for a long vehicle with its body so close to the ground is fairly apt, I am afraid some of the other code words are hardly as fitting. I referred just now to the conveyance of a circus and menagerie. The animals in one such consignment sent by G.W.R. consisted of cages of leopards, bears, lions, tigers and monkeys, and a few elephants. That family party was conveyed in sixteen " crocodiles " (for the wheeled cage vans), two " pythons " and a couple of " scorpions "; and the elephants travelled inside the " pythons " quite comfortably and without any loss of dignity, I believe. A " python," you see, is a covered carriage truck, and a " scorpion " an open carriage truck.

You may not be aware that of six thousand million letters handled annually by the Post Office, about eighty per cent. (contained in about twenty-five million mail bags) are carried by the railways. That's one more of the many services which the railways perform year in and year out, about which the country knows little.

So important, however, is this job of mail conveyance that special Post Office trains are run in which the letters

120-ton "Crocodile" Truck with interchangeable well (top) and straight girder sections

are sorted *en route* by a travelling staff. As these trains run at express speed mail exchange apparatus, by which bags of mails are put off and picked up at speed as the train proceeds, is provided at suitable places along the track. This consists of a " wayside net " fixed to the ground, which receives bags of mails suspended from an arm extended from the side of a mail van, or a " wayside standard " erected from the ground on which mail bags are hung and projected into the mail van by a net extended from the side of the van. In some instances a combination of the two, the net and the standard, is provided. The apparatus on the Post Office van is very similar to that alongside the line.

The mail-catching net in the Post Office van is swung outwards by lowering a lever in the van and simply dislodges and catches the pouches of mails hung on the arms of the wayside standard. The despatching apparatus from the mail van operates in the reverse way, of course. The despatching " arms " are near floor level of the van, and are swung outwards and their pouches caught in the wayside net.

The exchange posts are located by special lights and board indicators. When an exchange is in progress a warning bell is rung in the van as the pouches, which weigh about 50-60 lbs., come hurtling in at a pretty good pace. The exchanges are quickly made and the arms of the van apparatus then fold inwards and the collecting net collapses against the side of the van.

This apparatus seems to be a constant fascination to young railway enthusiasts, and I fancy they speculate as to what would happen if the collecting net was inadvertently

Special Train of 25 Admiralty Buoys on G.W.R. " Crocodile " Trucks

spread at a station and a few bookstall boys and other treasures caught up in the " trawl " ; but *that* would never happen as the net is only extended for a short time at certain well defined " posts."

In the handling of ocean mails, the Great Western Railway plays a prominent part, and some remarkably fast running is made with Ocean Mails Specials. At Plymouth several shipping lines make their first call in this country, and mails are taken off by fast tenders of the Great Western Railway and despatched post-haste to London and the larger provincial centres.

The Postal Authorities are in touch with the incoming liners by wireless, and as they near our shores G.W.R. tenders arrive the ocean mails special train is standing with postal officials and take off the bags of mails. As soon as these are checked, the tenders turn portwards and make all speed for Plymouth Docks, and by the time the tenders arrive the ocean mails special train is standing alongside to receive the mails, which are loaded by an electrically-operated conveyor from the tenders to the

train. As one van is filled the train moves forward and another is loaded, and this goes on till the whole of the carefully checked freight is aboard the train.

Meanwhile, a powerful locomotive of the " King " or " Castle " class has arrived and been connected up and is snorting impatiently to be off. About four hours, or less, after she gets the " right away " those mails will have been rushed across the 227 miles that separates Plymouth Docks from Paddington Station and there handed over to the G.P.O. for delivery.

∽   ∽   ∽   ∽

If there is one thing we all take for granted in these days, perhaps, it is that the newspaper should be delivered by the time we come down to our eggs and bacon in the morning. The expectation is just the same whether we reside in Reading or Redruth, Pinner or Plymouth—and we are not disappointed. In fact, we get our newspapers with such unfailing regularity that we probably never think much about how they come.

In the distribution of news, like so many other things,

163

the railways play a principal part. The London dailies are handed to the railways when the people of this country are normally in dreamland and it is the business of the railways to see that they arrive at their respective destinations—be they hundreds of miles away—when that sleeping population begins to rouse itself for another day's activity.

You have seen Paddington Station by day, but to

appreciate the organisation behind the distribution of newspapers you should be there just after midnight. From then until 2.0 a.m. over 100 newspaper motor vans run into the station and leave about 145 tons of London daily papers, while in the early hours of Sunday morning about 330 tons of newsprint are despatched by train.

The motor vans of the big dailies, each in its distinctive colouring and lettering, race from the printing presses to the station when the ordinary street traffic of London is practically stilled. On reaching the station their double doors are flung open and the bundles of newspapers,

Transferring Ocean Mails from Tender to Train at Plymouth Docks

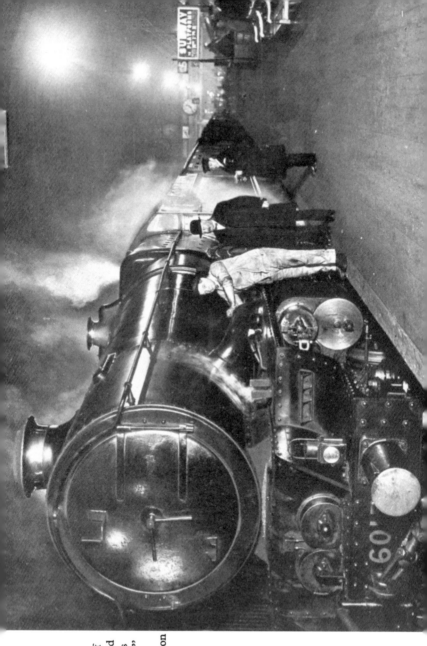

West of
England
"News
Special"
at
Paddington

addressed and labelled, are quickly transferred to four-wheeled trollies, weighed and checked, and passed into the long, well-lighted open vans of the newspaper train, where they are loaded, each in a particular spot, where they can be most conveniently unloaded at their various destinations *en route.*

Many of the trains conveying newspapers are "specials" for this traffic. The 12.50 a.m. from Paddington, believed to be the fastest newspaper train in the world, runs " non-stop " to Plymouth where it arrives at 4.50 a.m. (four hours only) and on to Penzance, serving the principal points along the route in Cornwall.

The 1.40 a.m. conveys newspapers to Taunton, Exeter and Newton Abbot, while the 2.30 a.m., the newspaper train for Bristol, serves a wide area and takes vans, detached on the way for Oxford, Swindon and Gloucester, and the 12.55 a.m. serves various destinations in South Wales.

All these and many other trains leave Paddington in the very early hours of the morning when the station is literally a hive of activity—particularly when events of national importance are pending and the printing presses have to include items of last-minute news. Still, they get the newspaper trains away on time and those whistling paper-boys manage to slip them through the letter-boxes before most of us are down to receive them.

ᔕ   ᔕ   ᔕ   ᔕ

I am afraid we have been so keen on our freight trains, mails, and newspaper specials that we have failed to notice the fact that we are practically at our destination. . . . There are the brakes going on, and this is Swindon Station.

Aerial
View of
part of
Locomotive
Works,
Swindon

CHAPTER THE SIXTEENTH

SWINDON

BUILDING LOCOMOTIVES AND CARRIAGES—MILK TRANSPORT— THE "WHEEL TAPPER"

YES, this is Swindon—the town on the hill —mentioned in the Domesday Book, which was a small and ancient market town when the railway reached it in 1840. That was the year before the completion of the original Great Western Railway from London to Bristol.

Swindon seems to have commended itself as the site for a central repair depôt for engines and other rolling stock about that time, for in February, 1841, the Directors authorised the construction of the works which came into regular working about two years later.

What the coming of the railway has meant to Swindon can be measured by the growth in population of the town. In 1841 census returns showed a total of 2,459 inhabitants, whilst the figure for 1931 (ninety years later) was 65,000. The number of employees at Swindon Works in 1876 was 4,500 and to-day is about 12,000.

The principal business of this town is the construction, repair and maintenance of the locomotives, passenger vehicles and mineral and merchandise wagons of the Great Western Railway. A pretty big undertaking, and it is difficult to visualise such an amount of rolling stock, but perhaps you will get a better idea of it when I tell you that the vehicles if placed end on end on both Up and Down Main Lines on the " Cornish Riviera Express " route would extend from Paddington to somewhere about Bodmin Road Station in Cornwall.

While we are on statistics you might like to know that Great Western Railway engines in a normal year run about 95 millions of miles, or a daily average equal to ten trips round the world. The locomotives consume about $1\frac{3}{4}$ million tons of coal and 750,000 gallons of lubricating oil annually.

Besides the building and repair of rolling stock, a large amount of general and miscellaneous work is performed at Swindon for the various departments of the undertaking, principally in the production of castings, forgings, etc., in the repair of machinery, and in the making of station and office furniture, etc., etc.

The big family of railway workers employed at Swindon are catered for by an extensive welfare organisation, which embraces a Mechanics' Institution with a lending library of 50,000 volumes, reading and recreation rooms, a large hall for theatrical and other entertainments, and a lecture hall. There is a medical fund society which provides medical and surgical attendance for 40,000 to 45,000

BUILDING LOCOMOTIVES AND CARRIAGES

persons (workers and their dependants) and has its own Turkish and swimming baths, well-appointed dispensary, and dental departments.

An interesting feature in connection with the Swindon Works Staff is the annual holiday which takes place early in July, when 27,000 people (workmen and their families) are conveyed in G.W.R. trains (free of cost) to various seaside and other holiday resorts. The holiday arrangements are a triumph of organisation in which every participant gets with his or her ticket, the number of the train, time and place of departure, etc.—for the station is inadequate to deal with such an exodus and the trains are started from various parts of the premises.

During " trip week " Swindon, normally a busy and active township, is almost deserted. The familiar sirens for starting work and " knocking off " are silent, the roar of the works machinery is stilled, the great chimney shafts cease from smoking and for one week silence reigns over what is normally a veritable hive of industry, while its workers make holiday.

Now let's go to the end of the platform and spy out the land. . . . Standing with our backs to London we are looking roughly westwards and you now see a good portion of Swindon Works in front of you on both sides of the line.

The Locomotive Works are on your right front, being situated on the north side of the main line to Bristol and the West of England, and the largest and principal of the locomotive shops—"A" shop—is the farthest away from us here.

The Carriage Works are those over on the south side of the line—on our left front now, whilst the Wagon Works

Another
View of
the
Locomotive
Works,
Swindon

BUILDING LOCOMOTIVES AND CARRIAGES

lie to the north-east, the nearest to the station on the north side of the line.

Before we start on our expedition there is another G.W.R. institution to which I should like to introduce you. It will fortify you for your afternoon jaunt, I hope—the Swindon Station Refreshment Rooms. Let's go inside and see what they can give us for lunch. . . .

∽ ∽ ∽ ∽

You will probably be surprised to hear that from 1842 to 1895 all trains had to make a compulsory ten minutes stop at this station. It came about in this way : Under the terms of leasing the Swindon Junction Hotel and Refreshment Rooms, the far-seeing lessees had secured an extraordinary provision that all trains should make a stop of ten minutes at Swindon for refreshments. What is more, this arrangement (if you please) was to run for ninety-nine years !

What hopes ? I ask you. Well, as you can imagine, the arrangement became unbearable to a railway always eager to accelerate its services, and in 1895 the Great Western Railway Company bought out the hotel company, and the price the Railway had to pay was no less than the refund of the latter's original capital of £100,000. A pretty high figure indeed, but it enabled much needed speeding-up to be effected between London, Bath and Bristol and the West of England generally, and now, instead of that compulsory stop and alighting of passengers for refreshment, they take their meals in all the more important trains, many of which pass this station at high speed.

Well, here's the menu—choose your fare and get busy,

173

for we have a walk through the Swindon Workshops before us this afternoon. Those works, by the way, cover about 310 acres (we are not going over them *all* this afternoon !), of which 65 acres are roofed.

You will see locomotives and carriages in course of erection, so perhaps a preliminary word or two may help you.

A new type of railway locomotive, or an improvement on an existing one, like every innovation, has its first existence in the mind of the man who plans it. The thought of the locomotive engineer has to be materialised, and the first step is to prepare scale drawings of the engine. These have to be accurate to the highest possible degree, and when finally approved what are known as shop drawings are made of the various components, which are manufactured by skilled workmen of many different grades.

Then patterns, templates, and other aids to the manufacturing of parts such as castings, forgings and pressings have to be made—also " jigs " to simplify the process of repetition work. Frames, plates, boiler, cylinders, motion, brake-gear, brasswork, etc.—all are proceeded with in the several departments, so that the various parts may be ready as and when required by the erecting shop.

As we shall see, the actual building of a locomotive takes place in a large shop over pits, which enable the workmen to get beneath the engine. Overhead are gigantic traversing cranes which are capable of lifting a complete locomotive over others in course of construction.

First of all the frame plates already drilled and slotted as required are set out on stands, and the cylinders put in position, correctly aligned, and bolted to the frames.

BUILDING LOCOMOTIVES AND CARRIAGES

Stays and brackets for carrying the boiler are next added, and axle boxes fitted.

The next contribution to our engine is from the boiler-makers. Having thoroughly tested the boiler, which comes to the erecting shop with its firebox and smokebox attached, it is " lagged," *i.e.*, covering it with asbestos material, over which are fixed circular steel plates. The boiler is now mounted in position between the frames to which are also fitted the motion bars and other brackets.

The pistons are now fitted, cab plates and fittings added, and then the engine is lifted by means of an over-head crane, and " wheeled," *i.e.*, its wheels are placed under it. The brake work is next fitted and numerous connections and adjustments made.

Now enter the painters, who, after giving the locomotive several coats of paint which are all in turn " rubbed down," apply a final livery in the standard G.W.R. colouring, which is then varnished. By the time the last coat of varnish has been added and various other small jobs have been completed, our locomotive is ready for her preliminary trials.

You will also see railway carriages under construction. In the earliest days, the poor third class railway passengers had to put up with many discomforts, for at first there were no roofs to protect them from the weather, and only plain hard wooden seats.

To-day, railway carriages are comfortably upholstered, well lighted, ventilated and warmed, while for long journeys there are corridor coaches with lavatory compartments, dining cars, sleeping accommodation, and so on.

The floor of the modern railway coach is made of deal boards with a covering of fire-resisting composition and

Train of Milk Tank Trucks

the sides and roofs are of steel fitted in a skeleton frame-work of timber, so that the exteriors are entirely fireproof.

Sixty feet is the usual length of the main line railway coach, although on the Great Western Railway there are some as long as 73 ft. 6 ins. Vestibules and gangways enable the train to be traversed from end to end. The equipment includes the generator and dynamo for providing electric lighting, automatic vacuum brake apparatus, hot and cold water supplies, and steam heating pipes and radiators.

When the framework and steel sheeting is completed, the upholsterers and trimmers fit the seats, armrests, and the like. They are followed by painters and varnishers who tackle the exterior and interior, and the glass is then set in the windows. At about this stage the coach is " wheeled," and after that the electric generator is added,

and the brake gear. When this has been done, the coach receives its final painting and varnishing externally, and the last touches to the interior decoration are generally added, including luggage racks, mirrors, and framed views of beauty spots in the railway territory.

These few brief preliminaries will, I think, save some breath for us when we get into the shops, for there, with the running machinery of all sorts it is not quite so easy to converse as it is here.

ᔆ   ᔆ   ᔆ   ᔆ

Coffee? Here's the milk; by the way, when you add milk to your tea, coffee or porridge at home, I wonder if you ever stop to think of the organisation that puts fresh milk on the Londoner's breakfast table every morning? In the case of the country towns the supply is of course, a simpler proposition, but little or no milk can be produced in or about London, although some millions of gallons are regularly consumed.

The Londoner, and for that matter, every other dweller in a big city, expects his milk *fresh*, and he gets it, though it may have been transported hundreds of miles. How is it done?

Well, in recent years there has been a great speeding up in the methods of milk supply, and three of the most important features are the large collecting depôts in the milk-producing districts, the use of rail tanks, and rapid transport.

The old milk churn, so familiar to us all at railway stations, now used less and less for rail journeys, is being replaced by 3,000 gallon glass-lined tanks mounted on railway undercarriages and equipped for fast running. The tanks are fitted with an outlet cock at each end, and manhole, air cock, safety and inlet valves at the top. Steps to the manhole and valves are provided at each side of the tanks which are cased in layers of cork two inches in thickness to check vibration, and covered in thin metal sheets welded together.

Three railway vans would be required to transport the quantity of milk contained in one of these tanks, under the old methods in churns loaded into railway vans, and the saving in deadweight haulage alone is about 58 tons!

Much of the milk consumed in London comes from considerable distances—from farms as far away as Cornwall, for instance, and it is modern methods of treatment and transport that puts fresh Cornish milk on the Londoner's breakfast table.

Road Milk Tank loaded on Rail Truck

The milk is collected by railway lorries in the familiar churns and these lorries leave empty churns when collecting the full ones. The milk is then brought to a central depôt where it is poured from the churns into a tank, cooled, and then conveyed by pipe to the glass lined railway tank wagons waiting to receive it, and as soon as these are filled they are despatched to London or other destinations.

Some of the milk is handed to the railway in specially constructed road milk-tank trailers and railway trucks are provided for transporting these vehicles. These rail trucks are fitted with elevated tracks and the road trailers have cast steel drums fitted on the insides of all the wheels.

As the trailer is drawn on to the rail truck from an end loading bank or platform (over hinged metal flaps which bridge the gap across the buffers) these drums wheel on to the elevated tracks and take the whole of the weight of the tank trailer and its load of 2,000 gallons of milk. The rubber tyres are relieved of the whole of this weight

179

owing to the falling level of the floor of the truck.

The trailer is drawn on to the truck by means of the wire rope by which it is hauled on the road. One end of this rope is connected to the trailer, thence round a pulley at the opposite end of the truck, the other end of the rope being connected to the road tractor, which is used to haul the trailer. Also, in position on the truck the trailer is secured with chains and wheel-bars.

On arrival at destination the milk is unloaded from the glass lined tanks at the rate of 150 gallons a minute by means of compressed air being filtered in the process. Every drop is pasteurised for safety's sake, being raised to a temperature of 145 deg. Fahr. and held to that heat for 30 minutes, after which it is quickly cooled and immediately bottled.

Now the deliveryman takes the bottles on his van and proceeds to deliver it at our doors, where it arrives fresh and pure for our morning meal. Milk-oh !

There's no need for us to hurry unduly in getting to the Works, for they will hardly be expecting visitors there for a little while. So, if you are quite refreshed, we will have a prowl along the platform and see what is to be seen.

The signals for the Up Main Line are off and here comes a flyer through the station on the Up road. That will be the 12.30 p.m. from Newport to Paddington, due to pass here at 1.45 which, you see, is the exact time by the station clock. . . . She must be doing a good turn of speed, for she is already nearly out of sight, and you will notice that the signals behind her have gone back to the " danger " position.

3,000-gallon Glass-lined Milk Tank Truck

You are interested, I see, in that man who is tapping carriage wheels with his long-handled hammer. He is a train examiner although perhaps more familiarly known as a "wheel-tapper"—a title, by the way, which you may recognise, for it has inspired a good story and also a fine song. The story is, however, quite libellous, for a train examiner has a very responsible position. He has to see that the working parts of carriages or wagons—wheels, axles, springs, brakes, heating apparatus, etc., are in good condition. By "tapping" the wheels he knows from experience by the "ring" of the metal that the tyres are in sound condition and not working loose. He is also responsible for seeing that the vehicles he examines are all properly lubricated. In fact, he is very much more than a wheel-tapper although that's the name that seems to stick. . . .

Now I think we had better be moving towards the Works—" the birthplace of the ' Kings '." . . .

The Saw Mill

SWINDON WORKS — CARRIAGE SHOPS

THINK, perhaps, it will be more convenient and save our legs if we enter the works by Sheppard Street entrance and take some of the Carriage Shops first, and then cross over to the north side of the main London-Bristol line to the Locomotive Shops. We can only visit a selection of the shops in the time at our disposal, but we will make that selection as interesting and typical as we can. . . .

They get a lot of distinguished visitors (besides your good self) at Swindon Works. Here come monarchs, engineers, scientists, members of learned societies of all nationalities and railway enthusiasts of all ages, including thousands of schoolboys, and in all about ten thousand people visit these works annually. Every employee here is particularly proud of the fact that when Their Majesties King George and Queen Mary honoured Swindon Works with a visit, some years ago, the King drove the locomotive " Windsor Castle " (No. 4082), which hauled the royal train from the Works to the Station with the Queen on the footplate beside him.

Here we are inside Swindon Works and we ſtart our tour at the Carriage Shops. We do not visit the shops in the sequence of building operations but that hardly matters, I think. Our firſt port of call is

THE CARRIAGE PAINT SHOP

The carriages come here from the Body Shop which we shall visit presently. You see workmen engaged in preparing the ſteel panels of the coaches for painting and others, who follow them, painting the lower half of each coach in Windsor brown and the upper half in cream—the familiar G.W.R. colours, known, I believe, more generally, as " chocolate and cream."

This operation is followed by the sizing and gilding of the lines, and here are workmen affixing the coat of arms and creſt of the G.W.R. by means of transfers. The whole exterior is then given two coats of varnish. Look what a glossy finish this gives the finished coach.

The undercarriage, previous to being received in the Body Shop, is scaled and cleaned by wire brushes and receives two coats of red-oxide. After the body is put on the undercarriage, the outer parts of the frames and bogies receive one coat of black paint and one coat of black japan. The floor boards are treated with fireproof solution before being fixed.

If we had been here a few weeks earlier, we should have seen workmen busily converting twenty or more railway carriages into " camping coaches." These railway coaches, which are placed at seleated beauty spots on the Great Weſtern Railway for the use of holiday campers, will each accommodate six persons, there being two sleeping and one living or dining seation in each coach. What a

Trimming Shop, Carriage Works

glorious holiday that would be—camping without all the risks of wet tents or bedding which accompany temporary canvas quarters. A big demand has already been received for this novel holiday accommodation.

We pass now into this adjoining shop which is

THE CARRIAGE TRIMMING SHOP

As you can see at once, the principal job here is the upholstering of carriage seats. First of all the linings and covers are cut out by a machine in layers of about 4 ins. deep. They then go to the sewing machines (worked by women) to be made up, and are afterwards fitted with springs and the cushions stuffed with horsehair. You see seats in all stages from the bare wooden framework to the finished article.

Finishing Shop, Carriage Works

CARRIAGE SHOPS

Other articles made in this shop are blinds, signalling flags, towels, etc., whilst there is a section of the shop over here where you see canvas vestibule gangways, leather dispatch bags, window straps, etc., being made.

The next shop we come to is

THE FRENCH POLISHING SHOP

in which women only are employed in staining, " filling," and polishing the interior doors and decorative woodwork of the coaches. We will watch them at work for a moment or two before moving on to

THE FINISHING SHOP

where most of the interior woodwork of the carriages is prepared, such as corridor, lavatory, and gangway doors, quarter or door lights, frames for seat backs, panelling, luggage racks, and woodwork for electric lighting. We have only time to walk through, but in doing so we get a general idea of the many jobs performed here. You will notice there is a full equipment of machinery in the way of circular and band saws, tenoning, mortising, planing, sanding and moulding machines, universal woodworker, and multiple drill.

The large and spacious shop we now enter is

THE COACH BODY SHOP

and, of course, you need a bit of room for building such items as 60- or 70-feet railway coaches in quantities.

The process in this shop starts on the timber which has already been cut to shape in the Saw Mill. The timbers are marked off for tenoning, mortising, etc., and then pass through the various machines before being handed over to the builder for fitting together and erecting.

Here we can follow the erection of a coach. As you see, the bottom of the floor which is assembled first of all, has intermediate members of oak and the remainder deal boards. The side and end pillars and battens are next fixed, after which window lights and other rails are fitted. It is interesting to note that these rails are in one piece from door to door. Inside compartments are then formed. The partitions for the corridor are oak framing and casing boards. At this stage the doors, which are made in this shop, are fixed. Steel plate panels are then screwed on the outside of the body. The next operation is the preparation of the roof. The roof sticks, which are of oak, being bent to shape, the steel plate roof is then fixed by screws. Seat frames are then fitted. Finally, the body is placed on its under-carriage and run into the paint shop for painting and so to receive the finishers' and trimmers' work.

Here is an interesting machine which I want you to see in operation. It is for clamping the door frames together before the screws are put in. As you see, the pillars of the door and the cross members, which have been mortised and tenoned, are placed in that jig and are pressed together by four hydraulic rams. . . . Now the screws are inserted and the door frame is complete and ready for erecting. A speedy operation which without the machine would take quite a time to perform.

Interesting as all that goes on here is, we must reluctantly leave it for

THE SAW MILL

where we are greeted by the curious sounds of all sorts of modern woodworking machinery, circular and band saws, planing, mortising, boring, shaping, general joiners and other machines. The work in this shop consists principally of the conversion and milling of the timber required for coaches, wagons, and road vehicles. The timber, which is

In the Saw Mill

supplied in suitable thicknesses from the drying sheds, is cut to the size required by the circular saws; thence it passes to the machines for planing and squaring. Afterwards the scantling is marked off for milling for the class of vehicle for which it is required, then taken to the various machines for boring, mortising, tenoning, and grooving, and it is then ready for the coach and wagon builders.

These shops are run on strictly economical lines and no waste is permitted. The wood refuse is sucked up from the various machines in the Saw Mill to a bin in the Destructor House, and automatically conveyed into a furnace. The heat produced is used to raise steam in a water tube boiler, which is employed for shop heating, wood bending, etc.

And that is, I am afraid, as much as we have time to see of the Carriage Shops this afternoon, so—observing the slogan " Safety First " and making sure that no trains are due in either direction (Yes, all signals are at "danger") —we will cross over the London-Bristol main line to the Locomotive Shops.

The Iron Foundry

SWINDON WORKS—LOCOMOTIVE SHOPS

NTIRELY as a matter of convenience, we will start our tour on this side of the line with

THE IRON FOUNDRY

Here we see a different class of work altogether. This shop consists of this main building and a number of smaller ones attached which latter are used for housing the cupolas, patterns, blowers and core ovens.

Castings for locomotives, tenders, wagons and carriages, together with hydraulic cylinders, rams, etc., are made here. The foundry is equipped with three overhead electric cranes, two of 20 tons capacity each, and one of 10 tons supplemented by four 9-ton steam cranes, two electric and one hand crane. The general equipment consists of moulding machines, emery grinders for dressing, fettling drums for cleaning the castings before dressing and two electrically driven blowers for the cupolas. The

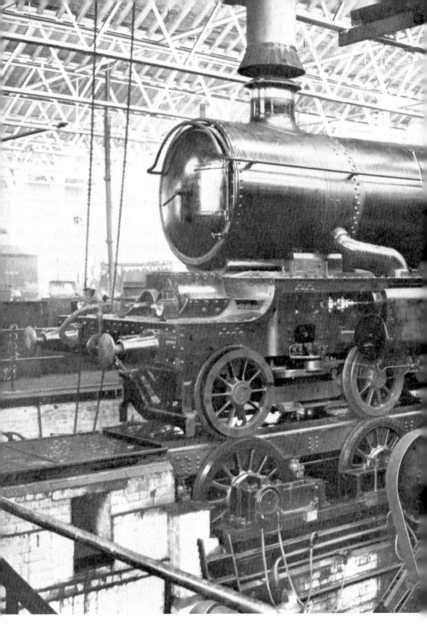

Engine Testing Plant

grinders and fettling drums are fitted with dust extraction suction plants.

You will, I think, be specially interested in the cupolas for melting the iron to be poured into the moulds. There are two of them and we will make a closer inspection of this one. As you see, it is a large brick-built furnace into which the raw materials, viz., pig iron, old iron scrap, coke, etc., are charged. These ingredients are conveyed in trucks which are hauled into position by hydraulic capstans on to a 20-ton hydraulic lift which raises them to the charging floor level.

The furnace, having been lighted up, the charging of the cupolas with iron and coke commences and when the furnace is filled to the level of the charging mouth, the blower is started. The two blowers in use are capable of forcing 9,000 cubic feet of air per minute against a pressure of 16 ins. water gauge. Air from the blowers is delivered to an air belt, surrounding the cupola and conveyed to the melting iron through openings called "tuyeres." Inspection covers, fitted in the air belt, enable the furnaceman to watch and control the working of the furnace.

Now what actually happens inside the furnace is this: combustion of the coke melts the metal above it which trickles down and collects on the furnace bottom. When sufficient has accumulated in the well of the furnace, it is tapped through the tapping hole and passes by way of a spout into a ladle.

We are fortunate this afternoon in being present in time to see the molten metal discharged from the cupola. Stand aside and watch it. Here it comes. . . . You see it is a white hot incandescent mass. It is poured from the cupola along the spout to the waiting ladle at a

Molten metal from a Cupola in the Iron Foundry

Pouring in metal to form a Cylinder Casting

rate of five to twelve tons an hour and is conveyed in the ladles to the moulds where the castings are made.

There are also a couple of Morgan Tilting furnaces here each of 600 lbs. capacity. These are used when metal of great purity is required for such parts as piston rings, etc.

But I should like you to follow that ladle of molten metal we saw run out of the furnace to the mould waiting to receive it. As you see, it is conveyed by one of the overhead cranes to the waiting mould and—here it comes —when in the required position the ladle is carefully tilted by the men on either side, and the molten contents are poured off into the mould. . . .

This particular casting which is being made is a combined cylinder and saddle casting for a " Castle " locomotive, and for its production it is necessary to arrange the moulding boxes in four separate parts together with 20 separate cores. To complete the mould these are added to each other and secured by vertical cotter bolts. For the final operation the completed mould is taken to a casting pit some six feet or more deep, runner boxes and risers are fitted and the mould filled with molten metal from the cupola.

Among other interesting appliances here are the coremaking machine and mills for grinding and mixing the moulding compound. The largest casting ever attempted and successfully carried out in this foundry weighed 65 tons.

On leaving the foundry for " A " shop we pass this 65-feet engine turntable, which is so nicely balanced that one man can by its aid turn the heaviest locomotive.

One-man Locomotive Turntable

Again we are in luck for here's one of the " King " locomotives—King Edward VI (No. 6012) coming on to the table to be turned. There she is completely on the table, and a pretty good fit don't you think? Now you see the man at the lever is able to move the whole 136-ton load and either to reverse the direction of the engine on the rails (as in this case) or, alternatively, to turn the engine on to rails set in some other direction. . . . There she goes. . . .

The secret of the easy movement of such a great weight is that the turntable revolves on a spherical centre bearing. This, and the perfect balancing explains why one man can move 136 tons so easily.

Now you see King Edward VI is heading the other way, and is moving off the turntable.

The vast building we have now before us is the famous " A " Shop—one of the largest and finest locomotive shops in the world without shadow of doubt. It has an area of over half a million square feet and is really a number of shops under one roof. It has been planned to provide for a progressive sequence of operations in locomotive fitting, erecting, boiler repairing, and wheel machining.

"CHELTENHAM FLYER"

We will commence our tour of " A " Shop by inspecting THE LOCOMOTIVE TESTING PLANT.

As you can readily understand it is necessary from time to time to make experiments on locomotives operating under working conditions and, by means of the Locomotive Testing Plant, an engine can be run at speeds up to an equivalent to 80 miles per hour, the wheels revolving, but the locomotive as a whole remaining stationary. This allows of complete observation being made at all times of the behaviour of the various parts. It also enables comparisons to be made of the relative performance of different locomotives under identical conditions.

We are fortunate in finding a locomotive under test this afternoon, for by watching you will learn more about this plant than I can tell you in many words. They are just starting up. . . . Now she is off on her stationary run. . . . There you are, she is coming to rest after doing a comfortable 80 m.p.h. and now we can make a closer inspection.

The plant consists of a bedplate carrying five pairs of water-cooled bearings. These are arranged to slide longitudinally by electric power, so that they can be adjusted to suit the wheelbases of different engines. The engine is run on the table of the plant, the flanges of its wheels bearing on grooves in the table, after which, the table is lowered and the tread of the engine's wheels revolves on the wheels of the plant during testing.

The drawbar of the engine is coupled up to a steelyard which holds the engine in position and registers the pull on the drawbar at the various speeds at which the wheels are revolving.

Such things as coal and water consumption, the analysis of smokebox gases, and ashpan and smokebox pressures can be readily obtained under easier conditions than would obtain if the locomotives were travelling on the road.

And now we leave the Testing Plant for

"A" MACHINE SHOP

where we are in a forest of machines, pulleys, and belts and amid the roar of running machinery ; so here, particularly, you must use your eyes and not rely too much on your ears.

The work done in this shop is the making of new, and repairing of worn, parts of the modern type engines, such as motion bars, pistons and rods, crossheads, connecting and coupling rods, piston valves, and solid and built-up cranks. Here you see many and various machines which are used to perform a host of different operations. Take a look at these crank axle lathes, on which huge roughing cuts are made with ease or the fine finishing cut which has to be very accurately performed to keep within the precise limits allowed.

Here batteries of smaller lathes are used for the lighter jobs, as you see, and—here again—as in all the work carried out in this shop, accuracy is the keynote.

These grinding machines are a most important part of the equipment of modern machine shops. They receive the work from other machines to put the finishing touches to the surfaces and work to a degree of accuracy which is not so quickly obtained on other machines.

Come and watch this plane mill at work on four coupling rods simultaneously. These machines are used for a number of operations, but chiefly upon coupling and connecting rods. After the rods are finished on the milling machine, they are taken to the buffing machine,

Planing four Coupling Rods

which gives them that smooth and bright finish with which you are familiar. . . .

These boring mills are used for axleboxes and piston rings, etc. The planing machines do many and varied jobs such as planing built-up crank webs, axleboxes, etc., whilst these drilling, slotting and broaching machines speak for themselves.

Yes, I know how difficult it is to move along and leave one fascinating operation to watch another, but we have much to see yet and I particularly want you to have a look at these flame cutting machines. They are used for cutting out blanks for various jobs. The cutting is done by burning with a jet, fed with oxygen at high pressure, and coal gas, and directed by the operator who, as you see, has to wear smoked goggles for his job. We simply must watch him for a few minutes, but, if we stay longer we, too, shall need darkened glasses, after looking at that bright steel-eating flame. . . .

There are many ingenious jigs and fixtures in this shop,

Frame Cutting by Oxy-Coal Gas Jet

had we time for a more leisured inspection, but we must move to another section of this big building—

THE BOILER REPAIR SHOP.

In this shop, boilers are repaired after being taken out off the engine frames. The operations consist of such jobs as putting in new or patching firebox plates, replacing firebox stays, retubing, etc. A great deal of work in this shop is done by compressed air machines, such as caulking boiler joints to make them stand up to the high boiler pressure.

Here, also, are machines for punching and shearing and plate rolls which can deal with the largest and thickest plates. What I do not want you to miss in this shop is this structure which carries the electric drills for drilling, reamering, and tapping firebox stay holes. The drills are suspended in such a way that they can be raised, lowered and moved left or right as desired. They can also be suspended at any angle to conform to the curves of the firebox.

A Corner of "A" Erecting Shop

RALPH MOTT

CHAPTER THE NINETEENTH

SWINDON WORKS—MORE LOCO-MOTIVE SHOPS

E next come to what is, perhaps, one of the most interesting shops of all, where the new engines are built and the old ones repaired. It is here that the famous "Castles" and "Kings" came into being—

THE LOCOMOTIVE ERECTING SHOP.

Here all the various parts of the engines are received from the machine, fitting, boiler, and other shops ready for erecting. The frames are placed on stands and lined up, when the cylinders and stiffeners are put in position ; then follow the boiler, motion, wheels, etc. The valves are set, the bogie placed in position and other small jobs done, then the engine is ready for painting. Before the boiler is put into the frames it is lagged with asbestos compound to prevent, as far as possible, the radiation of heat.

You can see some of the new "Castle" class engines under construction at these pits.

203

There is no need to go into the whole sequence of operations again as I briefly explained them to you at lunch time, but here you can see engines in all the various stages of construction.

In order conveniently to handle the engines in the shop, traversers and overhead cranes are used. The traversers —there are three of them, the largest being 42 ft.—are used for moving the engines in and out and about the shop. They haul the engine on to the table and traverse it to any position required.

There are eight overhead cranes in the older part of the shop, which travel electrically and lift hydraulically, and they have a capacity of 50 tons. The four you see in this newer part of the shop are all electrically operated and have a lifting capacity of 100 tons each.

These cranes can lift an engine complete from one position over the tops of other engines to another position —at the other end of the shop if necessary. The engine from that " pit " is to be lifted—let's watch the process. You see it is secured fore and aft by chains to the crane hook, then gradually raised (up she goes) till it is well clear of the other engines . . . and now, by a traversing action, the whole engine is transported some distance away and then lowered over an empty pit (down she comes— plumb over the pit). This " locomotive leap-frog " greatly assists operations without interfering with other work as would be necessary if a floor movement was carried out.

Each engine pit is supplied with compressed air which is used for drilling, etc., on jobs that could not be done before the engine is erected. There are also electric points placed about the shop for the portable electric welding

Wheel Balancing Machine

machines. The equipment for repairing is such that about 400 engines of large type can be dealt with yearly.

In the book, *The ' King ' of Railway Locomotives*, which I gave you this morning, you will find a detailed account of the construction of a new locomotive, which you may like to consult now that you have seen some of these engines being built.

Though we would like to linger round these locomotives in course of construction and repair in the Erecting Shop, if we are to complete our programme, we must now pass on to

THE LOCOMOTIVE WHEEL SHOP.

Here something like 6,000 pairs of wheels are dealt with annually. The work done consists of the building and repair of engine and tender wheels and includes tyring, turning, quartering, and balancing, and if you don't understand exactly what each of those terms means, you will in a moment or two.

The Wheel Shop

First of all you must know that the operations involved in the preparation of a pair of engine wheels are many. The wheel centres are purchased as steel castings. The castings are first of all put into a large boring machine, which bores a hole in the boss for the axle. They are next marked off for the keyway, etc., then placed on a keyseating machine and the keyway cut. They are then taken to the hydraulic press, where the axle (supplied accurately machined by the machine shop) is placed in position for the wheels to be pressed on. Suitable keys are then fitted and driven in.

The wheels, now on the axle, are placed in a turning lathe, which turns the rims for the tyres. After this they are taken to a gas furnace, where the tyres, already bored out, are heated and shrunk on, afterwards being firmly secured by a circular key which is rolled in place by machinery. The wheels are then placed in a lathe and the tyres turned to the correct dimensions.

Next they go to a quartering machine, which bores the holes accurately at right angles, to receive the crank pins, which are pressed in by hydraulic pressure. The gas furnace, which is used to expand the tyres for taking off or putting on, has the gas and air mixed in the correct proportions before entering a tubular ring which has flexible tubes connected to it. These tubes are connected up to the burners according to the number required to suit the various sized wheels. This ensures uniform heat round the tyres.

Now we will walk round and see the various processes in action. . . .

You will, I expect, be particularly interested in the large wheel lathe which prepares the rims to receive the tyres,

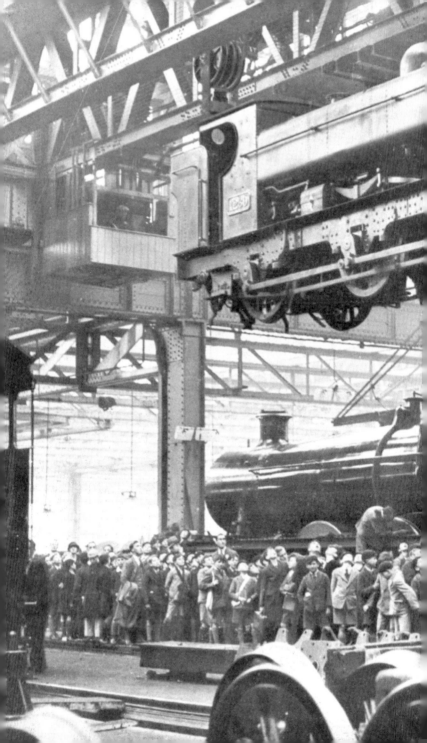

"North Star" and "King George V."

and in this wheel balancing machine which ensures the correct balance of each pair of wheels. Here are a pair of wheels being placed on the balancing machine. . . . As you see, they are turned at any desired speed, when the least inclination to revolve out of true is detected and the necessary adjustment made to the balance weights. It is this careful adjustment in the shop that gives smooth running and lessens wear and tear when the engine is on the track.

And now before leaving "A" Shop, there is a special exhibit we must not miss on any account. It is one of the locomotives acquired by the Great Western Railway in its earliest days, and one which was used at the opening of the line in June, 1838. "North Star" was constructed by Messrs. Robert Stephenson and Company for an American railroad, of 5 ft. 6 ins. gauge, but was acquired for the Great Western Railway and adapted to Brunel's broad (7 ft.) gauge.

MORE LOCOMOTIVE SHOPS

When this fine old engine ceased to be servicable, she was for some reason, not explained, broken up, but in connection with the Railway Centenary Celebrations a few years ago, it was decided to make an effort to rebuild her. Some of the principal parts were found here at Swindon and others contributed from all kinds of sources and—here she is.

" North Star " went to America in 1927 with the locomotive " King George V," representing G.W.R. locomotives ancient and modern, and both were exhibited at the Baltimore and Ohio Railway Centenary " Fair of the Iron Horse."[*]

When you have finished admiring the old " broadgauger " and comparing her with a modern " King " locomotive we will leave " A " Shop and go to the Boiler Shop, on our way passing through

THE BOILER STEAMING HOUSE

where boilers are tested after leaving the Boiler Shop. All types of locomotive and stationary boilers are tested here. The first test is a hydraulic test and the second a steam test. Steam is generated in a large boiler and supplied to the boilers under test. This avoids lighting fires in the boilers being tested, and enables the rivets, joints, and plates to be properly examined whilst under steam pressure.

Here we are at

THE BOILER SHOP

where the new boilers are made and it is without doubt one of the most up-to-date workshops of its kind. Here is a flame-cutting machine, cutting boiler plates to size, and the next process is the rolling of the plates into

[*]See " The 'King' of Railway Locomotives."

Another View of the Erecting Shop

cylindrical shape for the boiler barrels—that is done in these plate rolls.

The firebox plates are pressed to shape in this large hydraulic press, and when they come from the press, the flanges are cut off to size by a flame cutting machine. The internal copper plates are cut by hand saw.

The riveting, caulking, tapping, etc., for boiler stays, tube expanding, etc., are carried out in the same way as we saw these jobs being done in the Boiler Repair Shop.

You can both see and hear that there is a full equipment of drilling, punching, shearing, and other machinery in this shop. The boilers are lifted from place to place by means of these overhead cranes.

We next visit

THE CENTRAL BOILER STATION

where there are eight water-tube boilers which supply steam for practically the whole of the Locomotive Factory. This steam is used for hydraulic pumps, air compressors, steam hammers, steam heating, boshes, etc.

All these boilers have mechanical stokers and ash and coal handling plants. The coal is delivered in a truck to a rotary truck tipper, which turns the truck upside down and delivers the coal into a hopper. The coal is then taken by means of an elevator and conveyor to separate hoppers over each boiler; these in turn feed the mechanical stokers.

The ashes drop into hoppers which deposit them into a cast iron trough. In the trough, which is flooded with water, an endless chain passes along and pulls the ashes up into a ferro-concrete silo after which they are dropped into trucks and taken away.

The Central Boiler Station

The steam in these boilers is raised to a pressure of 160 lbs. and then passes on to a steam accumulator, which stores the steam that is not required at the moment and releases it when the supply from the boilers is not great enough for the demand. The accumulator also collects steam from furnace boilers in the Steam Hammer and Rolling Mill.

I think you will agree that this Central Boiler Station is a good example of modern mechanical handling equipment.

Adjoining the Central Boiler Station are

THE ROLLING MILLS

which were originally used for rolling iron rails, but when steel rails were introduced they ceased to function as rail-rolling mills.

Let's go inside and see if we can follow the operations carried on here.

The scrap iron received from the various departments is sorted into various grades, cut in those huge shears to the desired length, cleaned and scaled in a drum and then formed into a " pile " weighing about $2\frac{1}{2}$ cwts. The " pile " is then put into a welding furnace where it is heated for $1\frac{1}{2}$ to 2 hours, and is then withdrawn and taken to the hammer. The number of blows required to give the desired shape are from 100 to 150.

The pieces are again heated to a temperature of 2,700 deg. Fahr., which takes about 2 hours, and they then go to the rolls for shaping and are about 9 ins. by 10 ins. by 3 ft. by 0 ins. long in size. They are again placed in the furnace for another 2 hours, after which they are rolled again to the final shape required, cut to length by saw or shears and finally inspected.

215

Boiler
Shop—
Method
of
Staging

Steam
Hammer
forging
Connecting
Rod

There are three 70-cwt. steam hammers and 12 furnaces (ten welding and two puddling). The puddling furnaces are used for " balling " the turnings from the various shops, after which they are treated in the same way as the piles. The output from these mills is about 150 tons per week.

And now we are nearing the end of our tour, but we will finish up with a good smashing finale by having a look at

THE STEAM HAMMER FORGE

which is used for the making of large forgings, such as connecting rods, valve rods, quadrants, and extension frames, which vary from 2 ins. to 4 ins. in thickness and are from 12 ins. to 2 ft. 0 ins. wide by about 10 ft. 3 ins. long, and forgings of all descriptions up to about two tons are made here.

The forge is equipped with six hammers ranging from 25 cwts. to 5 tons. You may like to know that a full blow from a 5-ton hammer produces a crushing effect of round about 500 tons. A hefty smack that, but these hammers are under perfect control and can be so finely adjusted as to crack a nut without even bursting the kernel.

ノ   ノ   ノ   ノ

We leave the Swindon Works by the main entrance, which gives us an opportunity of seeing the Mechanics' Institution which I spoke about.

And now we must take steps—and pretty long ones—towards Swindon Station for time and " Cheltenham Flyer " wait for neither man or boy; so I must ask you to put your best foot foremost.   .   .   .

217

The Homage of Youth

SWINDON TO LONDON BY "CHELTENHAM FLYER"

E are in good time—3.48 p.m.—still three minutes before the Flyer's arrival. There is quite a number of waiting passengers and you will notice how keen some of them are in getting the porters to put the pictorial luggage label of "Cheltenham Flyer" on their baggage. We must get hold of one of these labels as a little souvenir of your trip.

The Flyer (whose official title, by the way, is the "Cheltenham Spa Express") leaves Cheltenham at 2.40 p.m., calling at Gloucester (dep. 2.58), Stroud (dep. 3.16) and Kemble (dep. 3.35), is due here at 3.51 and four minutes later leaves again at 3.55 on her "non-stop" run to London. . . .

Here she is coming in in grand style headed by "St. Mawes Castle" (No. 5018). As she comes gently to rest, many of the passengers gather round to admire the locomotive which is to take them at record speed to London. I think we ought, however, to make sure of our seats and if we can get them on the "Up" side so much the better for doing a bit of speed timing on the journey. . . .

This looks all right and there are vacant corner seats opposite each other—just what we want. Jump in. You

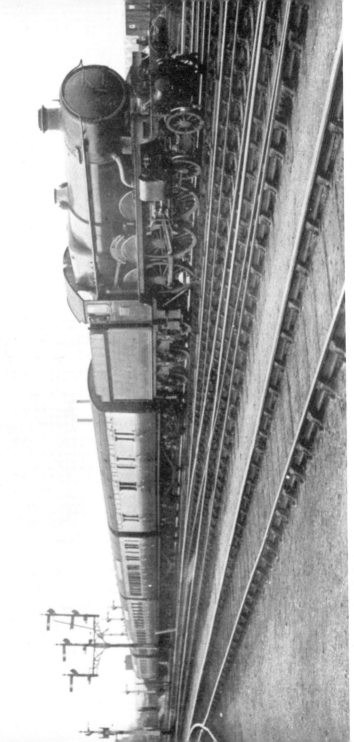

Leaving Swindon

had better take your seat facing the engine again, for from there you will get an earlier view of the quarter-mile posts.

Here are a few passing times of the train at some of the more important places, and we will keep this in front of us as we proceed :—

				Distance from Swindon.	
				Miles.	Chains.
SWINDON	..	..	dep. 3.55 p.m.	—	—
Didcot	..	..	*pass* 4.16 *p.m.*	24	14
Reading	..	..	,, 4.29 *p.m.*	41	26
Slough	..	..	,, 4.42 *p.m.*	58	68
Southall	..	..	,, 4.49½ *p.m.*	68	18
PADDINGTON	..	..	arr. 5.0 p.m.	77	24

There goes the right-away and that cheer is from the admirers round the engine. Gently we pull out of Swindon and notice that our watches say 3.55 p.m. to the very tick. A good start.

We are soon getting clear of the station, and speed is already increasing. . . . You will notice that acceleration is now steady and continuous and there is a feeling that " St. Mawes Castle " is getting into her stride. . . .

There's the 72 mile post (5.3 miles from Swindon) and we have passed the mile-a-minute figure ; in fact, are doing nearer 70 than 60 and still accelerating. Shrivenham Station (5.7 miles) is passed and still the pace steadily increases . . . we are now near Uffington . . . now we are through the station.

Here we might usefully try our hand at speed checking if you have got the table I gave you ready. You can call out when we pass one quarter mile post and again at the next, and between them I will check the seconds on my

Stop watch. Ready (" go ") one... two... three... four... five... six... seven... eight... nine... ten— elev... ("Stop"). Nearly eleven seconds. We are doing well over 80 miles an hour and nearer 82 or 83 I should imagine. That's pretty good and well up to schedule anyway.

On we go, faster and yet faster, taking Stations and villages in our Stride. The Steady rhythm of the train is punctuated by a whistle as we clear a Station, or a hollow sounding " whoosh " as we sweep under a bridge.

The landscape seems to be simply racing past us and the telegraph poles are surely placed much nearer together than usual. Although we are certainly laying the mileage behind us to some purpose this afternoon, the " going " is so good—so Steady and smooth—that it is difficult to realise that our pace is as high as we know it to be. This is speeding without any sense of haste or hustle, just gliding smoothly and swiftly at a pace which we see rather than feel, for it is the rapidly passing panorama which tells us the high rate at which we are covering the distance between Swindon and Paddington this afternoon.

I wonder if we had no idea of our speed, or that this was a particularly fast train, what our estimate of the pace just now would be. Far below what it really is, I fancy. It has been a comment of a good many who have made this trip that whilst aware that they were on the fastest train, they did not *feel* the great speed. That is rather a nice testimonial, I think, to the smooth running. Probably travelling at a slower pace on a less smooth track would give the impression of a speed a good deal greater than it actually was.

Now we pass Challow (13.4 miles) and Wantage Road (16.9) and the pace seems to be held if not increased. Do

" The Flyer " making history

you notice how the workmen in the fields stop to give us a wave ? The Flyer is quite an institution with them and, incidentally, a very useful timekeeper.

Here's Steventon, and now the Royal Air Force and Army Depôts we remarked upon when coming down, which means we have already knocked more than twenty miles off our journey.

Now we are through Didcot (4.15 p.m.) and we are one minute ahead of schedule here. I think I heard the tinkling of teaspoons and we might do worse than go along to the tea car and refresh. You should be ready for a reviver after your spell of sight-seeing. Bring your little speed table and we'll have another test. . . .

We will take this table so as to get a clear view of the quarter mile posts, and by their aid we can make another speed calculation after tea. . . .

When you consider the size of the ordinary kitchen used for preparing meals for a family of, say, five or six, it seems

little short of marvellous (don't you think ?) that in the small train kitchens meals can be provided for all passengers who may require them. The preparation, for instance, of a seven- or eight-course dinner for a hundred or more people—with all the various dishes and their trimmings—is a daily occurrence on most of the long distance evening trains. The cooking and serving is all carried out whilst

the train rushes onwards at anything up to 80 miles an hour.

This business of feeding the travelling public " on the move " is no small one. During the year 1933 the number of meals served in Great Western Railway restaurant cars was 1,300,502, including well over half a million luncheons, although " teas " were even more numerous, about 154,000 dinners, 86,500 breakfasts and 26,100 suppers. On a single

Power and Speed !

what 86 miles an hour means ? Well, 86 miles in 60 minutes works out at one mile in 43 seconds, or 123 feet in one second. Yes, that's moving, if you like !

Through Maidenhead and we cross Father Thames for the last time. Taplow . . . Burnham Beeches . . . and out there on the right you see Windsor Castle standing out bravely in the sunshine. Whish-sh ! and we are through Slough—at 4.41 p.m. (still a minute ahead of schedule) and pelting at top speed—Iver . . . West Drayton . . . Southall. Still no check; rather do we seem to be going faster, for here the stations follow so closely on one another, Hanwell—the Ealings—and Acton, and still no appreciable slacking of speed.

But now, after Westbourne Park, we feel a gentle application of the vacuum brake and soon we are coasting quite quietly as we pass Royal Oak Station and find ourselves gliding into Paddington Station and coming to rest at No. 7 platform. Let's hop out and go along to the engine. Why, look ahead at the Whiteley Clock we inspected this morning ; it's now showing the 4.59 indication, so we must have done our run about a full minute under the record schedule ! Bravo !

Our driver and fireman look very well pleased with themselves and so does " St. Mawes Castle," and all three of them have every reason to be for having made another successful run with the world's fastest train. As is usual, here is a little company of admirers waiting to receive the

Arriving at Paddington "On Time" —The Daily Record.

Flyer, and the customary ingredient of schoolboy enthusiasts is, of course, in attendance.

Well, we have come to the end of a pretty full day, and you have certainly heard and seen a good deal of railways since we left here about five hours ago. I hope you have enjoyed it all. You ought now to know something about railways in general, but I shall, indeed, be disappointed if you don't know quite a lot about the Great Western Railway in particular.

As for " Cheltenham Flyer," the subject of your inquiry, you have had first hand information, and experience, and I trust the world's fastest train has come up to your expectations. . . .

" Good going " you say? Yes, indeed. You know the comparative degrees of that phrase, I hope. They are—" Good Going "

" Better Going "—

" Going Great Western."

A U   R E V O I R

Pictorial Luggage Label in use on " Cheltenham Flyer "

A Song of the "Cheltenham Flyer"

I sing you a song of the famous train
   That's known as the " Cheltenham Flyer."
Little she recks of wind or rain,
   There's nothing that can defy her.
From Swindon she glides like a thing alive,
   Daily at five to four,
And at Paddington halts, when the clock's at five,
   Or a minute or two before.

———

Her steed is a " Castle," swift and strong,
   That comes of the self-same breed
As " Rover'' and " Hurricane," famed so long
   For beauty and strength and speed.
Her drivers must be of the very best
   To handle a train so fleet,
Such as Lewis and Bailey, Jones and West,
   Rudduck, Smith, Burgess and Street.

———

We're off, and the speed begins to rise
   As she gets into her stride.
The telegraph wires dance past our eyes,
   We're in for a glorious ride.
' Eighty an hour " for miles and miles
   Is her gait—and even higher
Mounts the speed—and our driver smiles,
   It's nought to the " Cheltenham Flyer."

———

Steventon's passed, we hasten away.
   Didcot lies before.
Over the points we tear and sway
   At " eighty-five " or more.
Pangbourne now. Of the river front
   We snatch a glimpse but fleeting,
And a man and a maid in a lazy punt
   Wave happy hands in greeting.

———

We've got the road, the signals down,
   We're travelling with a will,
And rush through Reading, " Biscuit Town,"
   With the whistle sounding shrill.
O'er Maidenhead Bridge we dash. In amaze,
   Turner would open his eyes
At " Steam and Speed " of modern days,
   And gape in mute surprise.

———

Slough—Royal Windsor leaping to view—
   Is passed, and we enter the maze
Of suburbia, factories old and new,
   Southall, and gramophone Hayes.
We've not been an hour, here's Acton now,
   But four more miles to cover
Seventy-three are behind us. That's how
   The Flyer can put them over !

———

Westbourne Park, and the goal's ahead,
   Our journey's well nigh done.
We enter the terminus gently : dead
   On time, and the race is won.
So here's three cheers for British pluck,
   To the train and her gallant crew.
We'll wish them God speed, and the best of luck
   To the old Great Western, too.

J. H. M.

(Reprinted from Great Western Railway Magazine)

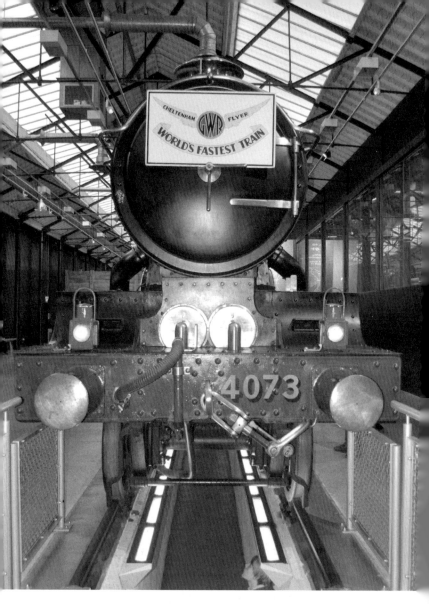

Built in 1923, No. 4073 *Caerphilly Castle* gave its name to the class usually known as the Castles. Withdrawn by BR in 1960, it is shown wearing the Cheltenham Flyer headboard at the STEAM museum in the old Swindon Works. *(No. 4073 photos by Jay Christopher)*

Cheltenham Flyer Revisited

It is eighty years since *Cheltenham Flyer* was originally published in 1934. This update section provides the opportunity to revisit some of the subjects covered and to assess how they have fared with time.

For the most part it is good news as much of the GWR main line has survived intact through the vagaries of the Second World War and the subsequent post-war nationalisation of Britain's railways. It is all thanks to the man in the stove-pipe hat. Isambard Kingdom Brunel did such an outstanding job in building the Great Western Railway that it has, as they say, proved fit-for-purpose to this day. When Brunel surveyed and built the line from London to Bristol he was determined to make it the finest railway in the world, and achieved this by keeping the gradients to a minimum and by building on a grand scale to accommodate his broad gauge. Alas the broad gauge was defeated by its narrower-minded rival but his railway line has been little altered, apart from a doubling up of the tracks in places to accommodate increases in rail traffic. It was not by chance that the London–Bristol line, or at least the London–Swindon section, was the one on which the Cheltenham Flyer established its speed records. It was also the first line chosen for the new HST 125s when they came into service in 1976.

The next major step for the line will see the electrification pro-

The Fastest Trains

The Cheltenham Flyer, as the Cheltenham Spa Express became known, established new records for a scheduled passenger service, which is not the same thing as an absolute speed record. As it is the GWR cheated by only measuring the speeds on the fast mainline section between Swindon and London. If the far slower part of the journey to Cheltenham – going from Swindon and up through Sapperton Tunnel and via Stroud – had been taken into consideration then there wouldn't have been so much to shout about. The GWR, however, recognised the publicity value in claiming such a record and pushed the average speed to 81.6 mph by 1932. The other railway companies were keen to claim a slice of the action. On 3 July 1938 the LNER's set the absolute speed record for steam when the *Mallard`* momentarily achieved 126 mph, a record that holds to this day.

Steam aside, today's travellers have become familiar with the notion of high speed rail services. These began with the famous Japanese 'Bullet Trains' in 1964, and since then many other countries have developed their own counterparts, including China, France, Germany, Italy, Taiwan, Turkey, South Korea and Spain. The longest network is in China where HSR – High Speed Rail – refers to any commercial train service with an average speed of 200 km/h or higher (roughly 125 mph). Over the last decade a government-funded building boom has resulted over 5,000 miles of HSR routes and they are the most heavily used in the world.

Britain's high-speed achiever is the InterCity HST 125. Introduced in 1976 the majority of the fleet is still in daily use providing the backbone of the country's inter-city services despite daliances with the ill-fated APT tilting trains. In 1984, First Great Western reintroduced the Cheltenham Spa Express name for its HST service and this departs from Paddington at 11:48 on weekdays.

Opposite top: Cheltenham Flyer headboard mounted on *Caerphilly Castle* at the STEAM museum, Swindon. *Middle:* The unmistakable lines of the Gresley A4, No. 4468 *Mallard*, at the NRM's Shildon facility. *Bottom:* Pencil-sharp nose of the Chinese HSR. *(wikipedia)*

Swindon Works

Swindon is a railway town through and through and the inter-war years were the heyday for the GWR and for the 'Works'. At its peak there were 14,000 people working there and the main locomotive shop, the A Shop, covered more than eleven acres of land. You only have to look at the photographs of the workshops – especially the aerial views on pages 168 and 172 – to appreciate its scale. During the Second World War Swindon Works was involved in the production of various types of military hardware, from components for tanks to midget submarines and landing craft. At the war's end it returned to the business of building trains, but this was the twilight for steam locomotives. In 1947 the Works turned out sixty new locos, but by 1954 this output had dropped to forty-two with only 200 produced between 1949 and 1960. British Railway's very last steam locomotive, No. 92220 *Evening Star*, was built there in 1960 and was withdrawn just five years later. Even before *Evening Star* had been completed production had turned to the new diesels. Thirty-eight of the D800 Warship class and D1000 Western class were built at Swindon between 1958 and 1964. But even as *Evening Star* retired the construction of diesel locos came to an end with the Class 14s.

Repairs, carriage and wagon work continued on a reduced scale until British Railways Western Region closed the Works in 1986. Since then the former works buildings have been put to other uses, housing a designer outlet village and the STEAM railway museum, while the engineer's office is the headquarters for English Heritage. On the other side of the tracks that other village, built for the workers and designed by Brunel in collaboration with Matthew Digby Wyatt, is still there. Rising up above the cottages are the Institute and the church – remnants of the inclusive nature of life when you worked for the railway company.

• See pages 168–217.

Opposite: Extrerior of the main offices, and some of the terraced cottages in the village built for the railway's workers.

Above, the original *Fire Fly*, designed by Daniel Gooch, entered service in 1840. Its 2-2-2 layout closely follows that of the earlier Stephenson-built *North Star* with a single pair of large driving wheels. These were flangless to create maximum contact with the flatter rails of the time. The replica *North Star* is displayed at the STEAM Museum, Swindon.

Relics of the Broad Gauge

The broad gauge was Brunel's great experiment to create a better railway. He spaced the rails for the GWR at just over 7 feet apart, more than 2 feet wider than the gauge selected by George and Robert Stephenson for the first railways in the north east of England. But condemned by Parliamentary Commission in 1846, and abolished in 1892, the broad gauge was also Brunel's greatest failure. Apart from the line, including some stations and several fine examples of goods sheds, very little remains of the broad gauge trains themselves.

North Star – shown at the bottom of the opposite page – was originally built by Stephenson for an American client and converted to Brunel's 7-foot rails to become one of the first locomotives to run on the GWR and it was certainly the first successful one. Withdrawn in 1871, it survived the great cull of broad gauge locomotives in the 1890s and was preserved at Swindon until 1906 when it was scrapped to make more room in the workshops, with only the huge 7 ft diameter driving wheels remaining. Perversely the full-size replica, now displayed at the GWR Steam Museum in Swindon, was created to mark the 100th anniversary of the Stockton & Darlington Railway in 1925 and it was wheeled out again for the GWR's own centenary in 1935 (one year after *Cheltenham Flyer* was published). This non-working replica incorporates the original driving wheels.

There are two other broad gauge replicas of note. In 1985 a working replica of Daniel Gooch's massive *Iron Duke* was created using donor parts from two Hunslet Austerity shunters. Built to take part in the GWR 150 celebrations, it is no longer capable of being steamed and is currently displayed at the Gloucestershire Warwickshire Railway's Toddington station in Gloucestershire. The third replica is the *Fire Fly*, an earlier Gooch design, completed in 2005 in time for Brunel's bicentenary celebrations in 2006. This runs in steam on a regular basis pulling replica coaches on a stretch of broad gauge track at the Great Western Society's Didcot Railway Centre. Clearly we will have to wait for the next big anniversary to see another replica. The only surviving original broad gauge loco is *Tiny*, a vertical-tank 0-4-0 shunter built for dock work. No longer running, this is displayed by the South Devon Railway at Buckfastleigh.

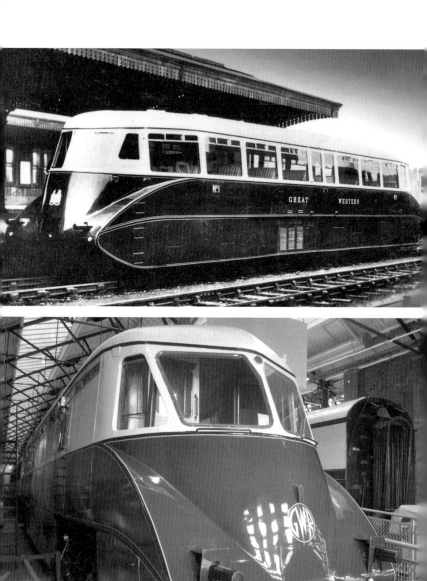

'Flying Bananas' – GWR Diesel Railcars

Inspired by the German streamlined diesel units, the GWR rail-cars were originally developed by Hardy Railmotors, a subsidiary of the Asociated Equipment Company (AEC). The prototype was purchased by the GWR and attracted enormous interest when it was displayed at the International Commercial Motor Transport Exhibition at Olympia in November 1933. The following month it took to the company's rails on the run from Paddington to Reading, and following a brief interval for modifications to the braking system and engine mounting it resumed operation with services from Slough to Windsor and Didcot. That same month an order went to AEC for six more railcars and these incorporated a number of improvements including a beefier 8.85 litre diesel engine, and three of the vehicles were fitted with a buffet bar to cater for the businessmen's service between Birmingham and Cardiff.

At the time of their first appearance the railcars seemed incred-ibly futuristic to a travelling public used to the noise and bluster of the steam locomotives. The railcar's 'air-smoothed' bodywork soon earned them the nickname of 'flying bananas'. Between 1934 and 1942 a total of thirty-eight railcars were built, with numbers 19-38 constructed at the Swindon Works. These later models had AEC engines of 105 hp. Seating for passengers ranged between forty-four to seventy depending on whether a buffet or toilets were installed. Two of the cars had no seats at all and were used as parcel carriers with a capacity of around 10 tons.

Three examples of the railcars have survived: Vehicle No. W4W, built in 1934, is at the STEAM museum, Swindon, and there are two examples both from 1940; W20W at the Kent & East Sussex Railway, and W22W which is preserved at the Great Western Society's Didcot Railway Centre.

• See pages 78–85.

Opposite: GWR Railcar No. 1, a cream and brown banana, plus the preserved W4W at the STEAM museum, Swindon. Ironically this is the only one of the three survivors not to have been built at Swindon Works. The later railcars had a far more angular bodywork.

Paddington Station

The London terminus for the GWR is in great shape. It has avoided the development creep that has blighted so many of the capital's high-profile stations, and in the 1990s Brunel's magnificent roof of wrought-iron and glass, arranged as three 700 ft-long transepts or spans, underwent a major refurbishment. The paintwork was restored to its original colour and in a weight-saving exercise the corrugated iron cladding was replaced with profiled metal sheeting and the glass by polycarbonate glazing. The long platforms have been cleared of years of accumulated clutter, including many cumbersome information boards, and there is new limestone flooring throughout. At the town end the 'Lawn' area has become an oasis of calm where the cappuccino-sippers can stroke their smartphones in peace caged behind a 150 ft-long glass screen. These improvements have restored unimpeded views of the curved ribs of the roof, leading all the way to the delicate tracery of the glass screen at the Country end.

In part this multi-million pound facelift was the sugar coating on a bitter pill. The second phase of the 'reduction and redevelopment' process was to demolish the fourth non-Brunellian span on the eastern side of the station. Added in the early twentieth century, the developers argued that although it loosely echoed Brunel's spans – albeit slightly bigger and constructed of sturdier steel not wrought iron – its removal was necessary to make way for a new Crossrail station. Its loss would return Paddington to its original, purest state. Hogwash said the many objectors to the scheme. The fourth span had been there long enough to become an integral part of Paddington, and its curving backbone had greeted generations of travellers descending the slope from Praed Street. Thankfully the campaigners got their way and the Crossrail station is now nearing completion out of sight underneath Eastbourne Terrace on the western side. Span 4 has also been restored.

- See pages 22–23, 35–42.

Opposite: Interior of Paddington Station looking down Platform 3 towards the 'Country' end. *Lower image:* First Great Western HST 125, No. 43146, beside a Heathrow Express Class 332 EMU 332012.

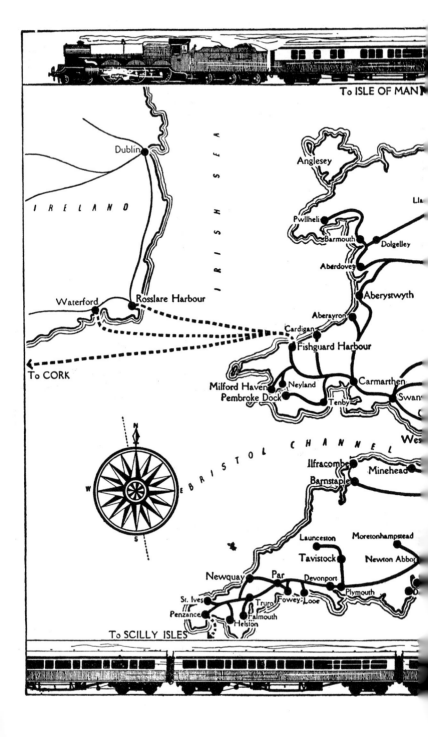

Also published by Amberley

GWR Track Topics

Originally published in 1935 – the year of the GWR's centenary – *Track Topics* is the ultimate railway book for 'boys of all ages'. Packed with the sort of fascinating detail covering the building and maintenance of the railway not found elsewhere, it is faithfully reproduced in its entirety in this special facsimile edition. Illustrated with over 200 photographs and diagrams, plus a supplement section to bring the topics up to date, it is the ideal companion volume to *Cheltenham Flyer.*

Price £12.99 ISBN 978-4456-2310-8

Cheltenham Flyer Acknowledgements
I am grateful to Campbell McCutcheon *(CMcC)* for providing additional images. Unless otherwise stated all new photography is by Jay Christopher or by the editor, John Christopher.